LEONARD SCHATZMAN
ANSELM L. STRAUSS

University of California
San Francisco

FIELD
RESEARCH

Strategies for a Natural Sociology

PRENTICE-HALL, INC., Englewood Cliffs, New Jersey

PRENTICE-HALL METHODS OF SOCIAL SCIENCE SERIES

EDITORS
Herbert L. Costner
Neil Smelser

ISBN: 0–13–314351–1

Library of Congress Catalog Card Number: 72–4469
Printed in the United States of America

10   9   8   7

PRENTICE-HALL INTERNATIONAL, INC., *London*
PRENTICE-HALL OF AUSTRALIA, PTY. LTD., *Sydney*
PRENTICE-HALL OF CANADA, LTD., *Toronto*
PRENTICE-HALL OF INDIA PRIVATE LIMITED, *New Delhi*
PRENTICE-HALL OF JAPAN, INC., *Tokyo*

Contents

iii

3

STRATEGY FOR GETTING ORGANIZED   34

4

STRATEGY FOR WATCHING   52

5

STRATEGY FOR LISTENING   67

6

STRATEGY FOR RECORDING   94

7

STRATEGY FOR ANALYZING   108

8

STRATEGIES FOR COMMUNICATING THE RESEARCH   128

EPILOGUE   139

INDEX   147

Preface

This book describes a mode of research and links its operations to the social psychology of the researcher, to the social situations in which he finds himself (both in "the field" and in his ordinary life), and to the logic of the inquiry in which he is engaged. Although the book is concerned with the method of field research, its principal focus is the field researcher himself; "method" is seen as an abstraction of the ways the researcher handles, or might handle, the many real situations, problems, and options which present themselves to him as he conducts his inquiry. By thus spotlighting the researcher, we avoid reiterating some standard fictions about research operations that scarcely resemble what field researchers actually do.

In the first chapter, we discuss a number of methodological and philosophical issues, through which we hopefully provide a perspective on field research and some understanding of its logic. In the process, we create a model of a field researcher who is at once a pragmatist, humanist, and naturalist. In succeeding chapters, we follow the researcher as he enters and relates himself to a human field in its natural state; that is, in its own time and place, and in its own recurrent and developing processes.

Throughout the book we emphasize that the study of something so real and so natural places in jeopardy many of the researcher's prior understandings and expectations of it; that much of the research process consists of dealing with a flow of substantive discoveries and with field contingencies that variously modify the research; therefore, that the researcher is constantly attentive to options which are circumstantially presented to him, or which are created by him. Thus, the field researcher is depicted as a *strategist;* for without linear-specific design—for the most part precluded by the natural properties of his field—the researcher must develop procedure as he goes. Accordingly, we have organized most of our writing around strategies: of entering, organizing, watching, listening, recording, analyzing and communicating. Finally, we cap our writing with a brief epilogue which tells why we have written this book.

Suggestions on Reading and Using the Book

Although some of the content of the book—particularly its sequencing—may suggest we have attempted a manual of sorts, this book is not, technically, a "how-to" handbook; it provides no complete list of principles or strategies from which a manual might be developed. It is entirely questionable whether one can actually be written. The properties of field research do not lend themselves to extensive prefabrication; natural fields and research foci and objectives are much too diverse for such an undertaking. Only through the reading of many books, monographs, and articles dealing with field research, and certainly through actual research in the field, will the reader be able to formulate an adequate conception of "all" that is involved. Then, he will be able to develop ways of managing the many standard and contingent situations that arise in this kind of work.

    Still, we anticipate that our readers will make varying uses of the book, including attempts at converting it into a manual. Whatever the use to which our writing is put, we recommend that the entire book be read or scanned first, and only later dealt with by chapters or by specific operations. In field research, most operations go on almost simultaneously—analysis with data gathering, interviewing with visual observation, recording with analysis, and so on; these are integrated activities. Thus, although we have developed separate chapters for the different sets of strategic operations, we would have the book read as an indivisible unit to help overcome whatever distortions in natural (to the reader) working sequences are engendered by descriptive, linear writing.

    Not only is it important for the novice in research to read the book as a single unit, but also for anyone with relatively little knowledge of social theory. We do not, in any particular chapter or section, provide sufficient explicit text in theory to make it obvious why we pose certain questions or make specific observations. For example, we discuss the nature of interviewing and even provide a schedule to illustrate how an interview might be implemented. However, we do not explicitly relate that schedule to social science theory. If the book is used as a text in a research course, the instructor—whether himself experienced or not in field research—will be able to help the reader relate procedure to theory, for example, to a theory of social structure. But if the reader is working on his own, then a full reading of the book will provide at least some of the perspective on theory we intended to impart.

Finally, a full reading of the book will help the beginner predict and rationalize the frequent puzzlement and frustration he most certainly will experience in the field. If nothing else, we expect that the entire book tells the beginner that he must expect to learn much about theory, about research, and about himself as a researcher *as he works out his inquiry in the field.* Really to understand this is to cut the sharp edge off frequent disappointments, and to help live through them. Experienced field researchers already know this. Most important, they know they are *always* learners when in the field, no matter how much they may be knowers. When the field researcher comfortably allows himself to become the learner, then he frees himself appreciably from the tyranny of self-imposed requirements to work flawlessly, without indecision, ambiguity, or error. Only a reading of the entire book makes this clear.

Some Limitations of the Book

Now, a brief word on limitations of the book as these may bear upon some probable expectations of readers: The variety of research styles, substantive interests, research objectives, researcher–host relations, and general field conditions under which these are expressed are almost as broad as social life itself. We could not hope to deal with more than a fraction of this variety. Hence, we have addressed ourselves to field situations, operations, and relations with which we ourselves are most comfortable and familiar— also to those we believe are of most general interest and usefulness. Thus, most of our discussion highlights research mainly into (1) established human-service institutions (such as hospitals), and to a lesser extent, into (2) nascent or relatively amorphous social movements. These two objects of inquiry offer many opportunities for study, either as whole systems to be researched *qua* systems or as sites which provide a multitude of more circumscribed problems for research. The reader will surely be able to relate the strategies and tactics we write about to situations and problems of more direct interest to himself.

Still other limitations relate to ethics and to styles, as well as to substantive interest:

1. The researcher model we depict is substantially an outsider to the group, organization, or institutional system he wishes to study. Though he may be knowledgeable about, or even a working participant in, the activity or world he wants to study, he is not so committed to it in his time and loyalties as to prevent his achieving conceptual distance from its perspectives and vocabularies.

2. Relationships between researcher and host are entirely voluntary on the part of both. In no sense is the host a captive to observation: the doorways to the site and to the various hosts there are opened through negotiation.

3. The identity of the researcher and the more general aims and method of the study are substantially known to the hosts. Our model researcher does not work "under cover." He accepts the obligation to make known to all classes of persons within the site who he is and generally what he is up to. However, he is not obligated to make known every detail of objective or turn of mind.

4. The general and immediate interests of the researcher are broadly scientific; that is, the researcher is interested primarily in describing, understanding, and explaining the activities of his hosts. All other interests are immediately subordinate to these. Thus, recommendations, evaluations or demonstration projects, while not precluded from later action, are not integral to the researcher's strategies and design. Even more remote are "investigation" and exposé.

We are aware that some field researchers work with different models and are not averse to accepting different purposes, strategies, or even different ethics. We shall not argue these matters, but simply assert that the relations we would establish with our hosts, and the purposes with which we would work, provide excellent conditions for gathering data. Of course, there are social situations and sociological problems whose study may require objectives and methods which the host, if he knew about them, would reject. We are not concerned here with such situations and problems, but only with those which can command the interest and respect of *both* researcher and host. Our model requires that the researcher attend humanely to the integrity of all his hosts, and to their requirements for freedom and trust, at least to the extent that he is capable of a degree of objectivity and tolerance consistent with his definition of science and his conscience.

We have not, then, attempted to establish a universal generalization on how all field researchers view and organize their work. Our discussion represents our own ideas and those of some close colleagues, with whom we share a perspective on this kind of work. Despite marked agreement among us on the nature of field research, nevertheless, there are distinctive differences in work style even among us, and in substantive interests, which inevitably yield variations in methodological procedure and substantive outcomes. The implications of this variation for reliability are discussed in our final chapter.

A note of explanation about the authorship of this book: For more than a decade the authors have exchanged views about fieldwork methods, as well as discussing their experiences in joint or separate research projects. This book, however, was written by Leonard Schatzman with close consultation by Anselm Strauss—who added additional points here and there to the original manuscript.

We are most grateful to our graduate students for their help in articulating the central ideas in the book; especially, Shizuko Fagerhaugh, Anna Mullins, Evelyn Peterson and Laura Reif. And for most valuable criticism of an early draft of this document, we thank our colleagues; especially Herbert Costner (University of Washington), Norman Denzin (University of Illinois), Berenice Fisher (New York University), Walter Klink (University of California San Francisco) and Neil Smelser (University of California Berkeley.)

1

The Logic and Social Psychology
of Field Research

In this chapter we identify some key components in the logic of
field research. We do this largely through an examination of the options—
decisions or attitudes—the field researcher takes on a number of methodological and philosophical issues. As the reader will see, some options may
be taken long before any particular research project is undertaken. We
make this point to sensitize the would-be researcher to the realization that
he may even now be making commitments to thought and work processes
he has not yet wittingly experienced.

The Concept of "Field" as a
Methodological Issue

Since we are eventually to tell how a researcher works in a field, we require a brief discussion on the concept "field" itself—not to define it formally, but to deal with a methodological issue inherent in the perspective
any researcher must take towards it. Academically, the term "field" refers
simply to some relatively circumscribed and abstract area of study. How-

ever, that particular sense gives no indication of how scholars operationally relate to their field; that is, *how* they study it. When we add the term "research," we get a qualitative change in its meaning: this adds a locative property, and while it does not exactly tell us what the researcher *does* there in the field situation, we may infer that he is not in a library or a laboratory—although we cannot be certain, for these also may sometimes constitute his fields. It should be clear that one does not know very much about the research as a set of operations when it is said that someone is engaged in "field research."

Our principal concern with the meaning of field research is that it *not* be taken as the functional equivalent of laboratory research. In the context of philosophies of research that offer experimentation as a prototype, the field may be taken for a facsimile of a laboratory. Although this is not how we look at it, we know that many otherwise sophisticated laymen, including graduate students, do. "Going into the field" sometimes conjures images of sharply circumscribed territories and exquisite control over a multitude of variables. Without arguing whether behavioral science experimenters achieve such control, we caution the reader against adopting this model. In the kind of research about which we are writing, this conception of circumscription and control is not realistic, nor is the search for them particularly fruitful. The field researcher understands that his field—whatever its substance—is continuous with other fields and bound up with them in various ways: Institutions necessarily reach out towards other institutions and are penetrated or overlapped by them; social movements are often barely distinguishable from the whole cloth they would attempt to re-weave. From the perspective of social process, institutions and social movements have no absolute spatial boundaries and no absolute beginnings or ends. Their parameters and properties are conceptual discoveries, and then, only for theoretical and practical working purposes, are they assigned boundaries.

For the researcher who is in the field the image of an experimenter in the laboratory is not a fit analogue. Not having done experimental research ourselves, we do not know what the experimenter does in his laboratory, but from much of his writing we do know what images of him and his work generally he would have us accept. These images do not fit the field researcher. He claims no antiseptic distance and noninterference from outside influence. When he enters the field, he does so with his skills and consequently with many of the situations, processes and perspectives—indeed, methodological biases—that link him with models of work and thought long since established in former training institutions and modified by experience. Also, when he enters the field, he maintains his links to institutions of current employment and association. Probably he is linked to kin and friendship groups which may affect him and his work through their mutual investment and obligations. Thus, both the field (or object within it) and the researcher are inextricably linked to other "fields" and social situations—any or all of which impinge upon his research. Indeed, the researcher may consciously use these as resources, as we shall point out in later chapters.

Problem and Method as Career Choices

Conventional wisdom suggests that a researcher prepare a relatively articulated problem in advance of his inquiry. This implies that he would not, or could not, begin his inquiry without a problem. Yet, the field method process of discovery may lead the researcher to his problem *after* it has led him through much of the substance in his field. Problem statements are not prerequisite to field research; they may emerge at any point in the research process, even toward the very end. Hence, although we were initially inclined to begin our discussion of field operations with a chapter on "Strategy for Problem Focusing," second thoughts led us to a different perspective on when and how research problems may develop.

If a problem can be developed late in the research, or immediately preceding it, can it not also be developed as far back as graduate or professional training—not necessarily as a distinct problem suitable to immediate research, but as a general orientation to the major problems in a field? Typically, in graduate education, much time is devoted to the theories and the traditions of the discipline. Research is usually undertaken long after the student has been saturated with the substantive problems developed by his illustrious predecessors. The student gets a kind of symbolic practice in the language of "problem formulation." Perhaps without his realizing it, he develops an approach to his discipline that may constitute a style of problem formulation, or at least a way of asking certain kinds of questions.

As an aside, for those students who may not have this kind of training—for example, those in the service professions—we would add the following: Since they also want to do research of a social science cast, but do not wish to spend years steeping themselves in the traditions of social science, we would say that it is entirely legitimate and practical to pursue their interests without the necessity for articulating precise problems drawn from the social science literature. Further, it is just as well that they have "only" something of a substantive focus, such as "clinical, interprofessional teamwork," and perhaps a few questions in mind that might be directed at the focus. Even then, some are practically unable to ask fruitful research questions, though they are certainly able to pose clinical ones. We urge them to go ahead and begin to observe in the focal area, assured from our experience with such students that given a modicum of intelligence, motivation, and experience in the given substantive area, they will discover properties in the observational situation that will yield questions and problem statements.

We think that a similar case can be made for methodology—when, where, and how it all began. Linear-thinking methodologists usually tell us that the choice of a research method will or should logically follow the formulation of a researchable problem. Indeed, this seems entirely logical, considering that a way of solving a problem usually follows its conceptualization. Yet, cannot the process be the other way around? In graduate training, methodology is taught equally with theory, but it is not unusual to find students developing methodological skills and preferences some time before developing theoretical ones. Considering the emphasis upon instrumentation, we find many students becoming methodologists in their chosen fields, and then in later years we find them searching for problems that are amenable to favored research procedures. This too constitutes a stylistic development. Of course, the same is true for students who develop skills in field research. Hence, we can look to the selection of *both* problem and method as bench marks in early stages of research careers, and in many instances we can locate the selections long before any given research has been undertaken.

Philosophical Issues and
Pragmatic Solutions

Other intellectual issues, though not strictly methodological in the operational sense, nevertheless significantly influence the development of research perspective and careers. Thus, a good education in his field will simultaneously confront the student with both mechanistic and humanistic orientations. The one leads to a search for explanations of social forms in processes independent of human definition and choice; the other tends to lead directly to definitional processes. Yet, though these orientations seem different in kind, not all professed humanists eschew the mechanistic orientation; some posit need structures or an "unconscious" as motivators of behavior, indicating that their humanism is little more than a profound concern for man as a value. But another form of humanism, more naturalistic in its interest and attitude, focuses, for study purposes, primarily upon man's symbolically shaped cognitive processes and sees in these processes the keys to human understanding and explanation. However these distinctions are made—more usually implicit than explicit—pedagogical emphasis favoring one over the others will profoundly shape student thought and later work.

Often without his realizing it, the student will also be confronted simultaneously with "structure-function" and "process" orientations. These will eventually pose epistemological problems affecting his definition of social phenomena—as real or conceptual, finite or infinite. Many students do not see very early, if at all, the broad implications of these issues for their evolving styles of work and thought. But when they do, they will find it necessary to take positions on these issues and then will begin to anticipate the implications of their commitments. Probably, some students will have to do some research before they realize these as issues at all. If they do not even then, their work will be eclectic or they will pursue research projects by whim or by "opportunity," with positions on the issues dictated by employment and funding agencies.

The naturalistic researcher with whom we are concerned in this book makes a commitment at some point in his career (the earlier the better) on the issue of mechanism and humanism. He opts in favor of the latter because he finds that the human scene exhibits special properties in addition to those which might be attributed to nonhuman contexts. These properties indicate a different order of thinking about man, and a different method for studying him. The properties are many and complex; to avoid writing an entire social psychology, we mention only a few which stand out as centrally significant.

1. Man can take a perspective on himself, and act towards himself.
2. In diverse situations, he can simultaneously hold several perspectives on himself as well as on other things and events—even seemingly contradictory ones, then in new situations create still other perspectives.
3. Personal perspectives are social in origin and emanate from definitions of countless social situations and processes in which man finds himself, and with which he can identify.
4. Man presents himself with perspectives and definitions that become (some of the) conditions for his own actions; therefore, the "forces" which impel him to act are substantially of his own making.

For the naturalistically-oriented humanist, the choice of method is virtually a logical imperative. The researcher *must* get close to the people whom he studies; he understands that their actions are best comprehended when observed on the spot—in the natural, ongoing environment where they live and work. If man creates at least some of the conditions for his own actions, then it can be presumed that he acts in his own world, at the very place and time that he is. The researcher himself must be at the location, not only to watch but also to listen to the symbolic sounds that characterize this world. A dialogue with persons in their natural situation will reveal the nuances of meaning from which their perspectives and definitions are continually forged.

It follows that the exclusive use of interviews or questionnaires poses methodological problems for the researcher who thinks situationally about the people he studies. These are fine tools insofar as they reveal people's constructs of themselves and their worlds as symbolically developed and rendered: people tell *what* they do and *why* they do it. However, two major difficulties flow from reliance—exclusive of observation—on these research techniques. First, any given person may be no more able to describe and explain his own actions than anyone else's: his vocabulary may be poverty stricken, or his perspective too difficult to comprehend by listening or reading alone (also, he may lie or "put on" the interviewer). Second, interview or questionnaire procedures constitute situations in their own right; therefore, what persons report in either case often better reflects those situations than the referential ones which the techniques were designed to ascertain. Referential situations are too quickly and readily converted by any given respondent into relatively idealized models when he is talking with researchers outside the "real" situation.

On the structure-versus-process issue, the model naturalistic researcher of our book opts for *process* as the more fruitful orientation. We shall be stressing throughout this book the implications for field research of this decision and shall not try to explain why he does so. Here we shall note only that at some point in his career, perhaps as a student, the researcher may come to see social relations not as structures that "perform" a limited number of functions, nor as structures which change from time to time, but as processes which from time to time may be dealt with as structures and which will exhibit a multitude of consequences. At some time in his career, perhaps while relating an ordinary but lengthy story to someone, the researcher may find himself using a homely phrase such as "in the meantime (or meanwhile)," thereby capturing some of the meaning of social process. For in that phrase there are indicated (somewhere off stage) events that inevitably cut across the "meantime" of whatever the story is about—group, person, institution, or idea—and that will alter an otherwise uninterrupted process. In a world where "all things being equal" are hardly ever that, the cross-cutting of multitudes of "meantimes" will yield ever-new processes and consequences which, from time to time, may take on the appearance of structures. One implication of this is that the researcher who understands this in the context of his research—that otherwise extraneous "meantimes" naturally affect *both* him and his object of inquiry—will probably be very pragmatic about his research operations as well as about the realities that affect them.

Once the decision has been made to inquire into some social process in its own natural context, the researcher creates much of both his method and the substance of his field of inquiry. To say that the researcher creates his method *as he works* may seem unbecoming, yet we are discussing this very point. Method is seen by the field researcher as emerging from operations—from strategic decisions, instrumental actions, and analytic processes—which go on throughout the entire research enterprise.

We are quite aware of another methodological tradition which regards method as "extant" prior to research. Instruments and strategies for their implementation are developed before the start of the research, and ideally are not refashioned in its later processes. The "variables" in the research situation are thereby seen as "controlled" through design. According to this perspective, scientific method is embedded in prepared design and in analytic processes performed "after the data are in." Yet one need not juxtapose this view against the other; if the research process can be thought of as *beginning* with a rough idea and *ending* with the publication of refined ideas, then it can be shown that similar, if not identical, processes are performed in all modes of original research, differing mainly in the sequence of their occurrence. In field research a refashioning of design must go on through most of the work. We shall show why this is necessary and how the process is regulated.

As with methodology so with substance. The field researcher views the substance or reality of his field in creative, emergent terms: it is neither fixed nor finite, nor independent of human conception and subsequent redefinition; therefore, it is not "all there," needing only to be located, measured and then rendered as "findings." He assumes reality to be infinitely complex—certainly *more* complex than any current rendering of it —and that he as an observer holds the key to an infinitely varied relation with the objects of his inquiry. Therefore, the researcher's developed understanding of his object is not necessarily or merely "true" or "untrue"; rather it is to be evaluated according to its usefulness in furthering ideas about this class of object and according to whether the understanding is grounded in data.

The field researcher is a methodological pragmatist. He sees any method of inquiry as a system of strategies and operations designed—at any time—for getting answers to certain questions about events which interest him. He understands that every method has built-in capabilities and limitations that are revealed in practice (through the techniques used, for given purposes and with various results), evaluated in part against what could have been gained or learned by any other method or set of techniques. Also, he understands that a method of inquiry is adequate when its operations are logically consistent with the questions being asked; when it adapts to the special characteristic of the thing or event being examined; and when its operations provide information, evidence, and even simply perspective that bear upon the questions being posed.

As a methodological pragmatist, the field researcher concerns himself less with whether his techniques are "scientific" than with what specific operations might yield the most meaningful information. He already assumes his own honesty, rationality, and scientific attitude; therefore, he is not ready to concede in advance the superiority of certain types of "instrumentation" over his own abilities to see and to make sense of what he sees. He is certainly aware of selectivity in human perception and of the probability of bias, but he does not view "objective" or "consensually validated" techniques as being free of these limitations either.

One of the authors recently joined an anthropologist and other social scientists preparing a grant proposal on American Indians' use of health facilities in the San Francisco Bay Area. The anthropologist had previously studied several Indian groups on reservations and was familiar with members of the same tribes living in the Bay Area cities. The site visitors questioned the research team closely on sampling techniques and alluded to its failure to circumscribe a universe. The anthropologist explained that no one knows such a universe, therefore random or stratified sampling is impossible. The site visitors asked why the Indian Bureau files could not be taken as the universe. The anthropologist replied that most Indians distrust the Bureau and that its files on Indian whereabouts are inadequate because undetermined numbers of Indians arrive in the area without checking in with the Bureau and because many who do check in subsequently leave without checking out. The site visitors understood the issue, but rejected the proposal on this and other such procedural grounds.

Still, where others may shrink from inquiries of this kind, the field researcher is prepared to invent method on the spot; this he does without qualm although with consideration of issues related to reliability and validity. Thus, having opted for problems best studied up close, in the field, he views techniques—indeed whole methods—not only according to the generalized requirements of science but also to the requirements of his research problem and the properties of his particular research situation. For him scientific method is not a prescriptive set of acts handled in the foreground of activity; rather it is a philosophical mandate to render empirically the relation between himself as observer and the observed event. Scientific method is part of the context within which inquiries are made.

Since the field researcher senses the great complexity of social reality and sees the operational relation between discovery and creativity, he is less inclined quickly to measure or test his findings—not because he fails to appreciate the need for "nailing things down" (they are, after all, *his* findings) but because he is never quite sure that his latest "finding" is critical or is the final one. More important to him than "nailing it down" is "linking it up" logically, theoretically, and empirically to other findings or discoveries of his own and others. Then, he may measure or test it.

Control of the Research Process

If our discussion of the research process makes it seem so uneven, so pragmatically organized and executed, how is it actually controlled? Most of the remainder of this book will attempt to answer this question. Prepared as chapters on strategies and tactics of operations, that answer will not directly deal with controls over research which emanate from less obvious sources. There are several orders or classes of control: some are visible and explicitly embodied in the research itself, others are less apparent, and some are not visible at all. Visibility is not the sole measure of their influence.

Not always fully apparent are the researcher's *guiding theory* or perspective, his *problem* or starting focus, and *hypotheses* or assumptions. Most explicit usually are such processes as sampling, scaling, rating, and testing. The latter aggregate of controls constitutes procedures common to many kinds of research, and is available to researchers for use at their own discretion. But the sources of this discretion are not visible in the published research and lie in other orders of control: in the researcher's education in science, in the institutional bases of his work—including the institution which employs him and the one which provides him with research funds—and among his intellectual colleagues. These last constitute the context—often the very reason—for the research, and directly impinge upon the researcher's career as well as upon his performance in the field. Contextual controls cannot simply "go without saying"; they require attention if only to dispel the notion that impersonal, instrumental controls embedded in the research are the only ones available to prevent the researcher's being victimized by his own biases, forgetfulness, error, and other threats to his objectivity and accuracy.

Some consideration of these contextual controls will facilitate later discussion. It can be presumed that during the researcher's university education, he learned about science as an attitude and as a body of knowledge; also, it can be presumed that he learned about science as a way of thinking and working. A good deal of his education emphasized scientific method and procedure. Indeed many university graduates learn their methodology lessons too well, becoming more adept at criticism than at original research or becoming gun-shy of public presentation of their observations except as "findings" processed through impersonal instruments. Through education into a substantive discipline and its methodology, the researcher comes to identify with the scientific community at large as well as with his professon, and develops a notable measure of commitment to scientific thinking. His identification and commitment have considerable stability even when he moves into and out of various institutions, occupational positions, and substantive interests.

Most researchers work in universities, government, or research corporations. These often finance the research, and in many ways directly influence specific projects, at times even dictating problem and method. There is some influence also by agencies that provide grants and contracts to researchers not directly employed by them. To gain agency support, researchers usually provide laboriously detailed agenda and rationale by which they promise to abide. Then, there is the task of writing—of enduring the tyrannical discipline required to communicate with professional audiences, and of anticipating the criticism, not only of "true colleagues" who think as the researcher does and who would presumably be relatively tolerant, but of those "others" who think and work differently from the researcher. All these audiences keep him alert to the relevance, usefulness, and validity of his work, for they affect his career as well. Agents of institutions and professional organizations, acting as employers, funders, publishers, and critics, tend to be invisible in the research and taken for granted mainly because the linear model of research provides no room for indicating their relevance, except perhaps as a strategic footnote acknowledging institutional support and affiliation. Yet these agents substantially influence the research, the researcher and his career.

Perhaps most important as a control over the research process is the influence of the researcher's intellectual colleagues, that primary group of scholars and researchers whose members are variously caught up in each others' work and careers. It might even be said that the research is addressed to relatively few persons in the discipline. These colleagues have, for all practical purposes, defined the field as a discipline, at least in its present form—its principal categories, problems, issues, questions, and its very history—and have given the field its main intellectual thrust or movement. In effect, research can be seen as a collegial dialogue—part of a history of relations between members of the collegial group and the known or presumed properties of their field. The colleagues share the triumphs and failures of the process of inquiry and exercise great control over it, through mutual aid and criticism, often more effectively before and during the research than following it. In this context, the colleagueship may be said to be the principal determination of the methodological styles of its membership, for it is this group that indicates most directly the propriety of its methodology, sets the limits of permissibility and legitimacy of research procedure, and establishes the standards of proof or of explanation. Through such colleagueship the researcher develops an orientation towards his discipline and his research as a form of work, and creates an image of himself as selectively interested in, and competent to handle, the problems and research processes of his discipline.

Relating to the Object of Inquiry

After induction and socialization into the history and categories of his discipline, the researcher pursues for himself some special aspect of its major problems and issues. Whether his own research is old or novel, generally it is formed from one or more of several basic questions (raised in all scientific disciplines) that are directed at some phenomenon—thing, person, relationship, process. What are its properties? What does it do, or how does it work? How does it affect other things and, in turn, how is it affected by them? How did it come to be? What is it becoming? In more formal terms, these are questions of structure, function or process, relations in a system, origins, and development or change. They can be raised in the context of description, explanation, or prediction. In the most abstract sense, all the questions can be thought of as part of a single definitional one: What is it?

Again, we offer a brief aside to those educated in a tradition more clinical than academic. Clinical orientations, rooted relatively firmly in questions of normality and pathology, perhaps lead too quickly to raising questions that focus on the restitution or improvement of conditions—not only the conditions of a natural pathological process, but also the practices and institutional conditions created to deal with the pathology. It is at the latter point that the clinically minded must concern themselves with some of the questions that we have raised. To implement changes in social conditions assumed to be inimical to health and normality, the clinician must ask, along with the more academically minded, What is it?

As the researcher reformulates for himself one or another of the basic questions, simultaneously he begins to formulate a way of working towards their answers. He is already familiar with several methodological models, which he learned in association with his teachers and coprofessionals. He can conduct experiments; survey a universe of objects; conduct a longitudinal, historical or comparative study; or "simply" observe and describe one object or a cluster of objects. Yet, the selection of a method is not so simple, especially if he engages in genuinely original research.

The procedures that he works out—some in advance, some developed later—are consistent not only with the questions asked and the methodological requirements of science, but also with the state of the science (its "software" and "hardware") in relation to the "presenting properties" of the observational situation. These more obvious or presumed features of the research situation "inhere" in the researcher, in the object of his inquiry, and in the physical and social relationship between them. Pertaining to the social science field researcher himself, we mean properties such as his initial attitude toward the object, the history of his relations with that class of object, his commitment to the research, his interpersonal skills, and his style of work. Social objects themselves vary widely in the properties they present: size, complexity, fixity in space and time, subtlety or abstractness of activities, and so on. The relationship itself between researcher and phenomenon is conditioned by physical properties such as distance, accessibility, and visibility, and by social properties such as the need for privacy and trust, or the degree of mutual interest in the research. Of course, in time some of the presenting properties become more important to the research process and some less so; some of the presumed properties are found to be nonexistent; and still other properties—neither initially obvious nor presumed—are later discovered.

The discovery process and the questions raised by the researcher need not be related to any "received" or prior theory. Such theory is not necessary to inquiry in the field, except when the researcher specifically wants to test one or explore the limits of its usefulness. The researcher is free to think of any or all pertinent theories and assumptions about his subject matter, and thereby frees himself from substantive orthodoxy. What he does need is some theoretical perspective or framework for gaining conceptual entry into his subject matter, and for raising relevant questions quickly. His framework need be no more elaborate than a scheme of general but grounded concepts commonly applied by his discipline. Without explicit theory as a guide, the researcher may relinquish some measure of control over the inquiry but probably he will make his relation to it more flexible and hopefully thereby generate new theory.

Nor is it necessary for him to work with explicitly formulated hypotheses, although of course he may wish to test an existing one. (He may have to in order to satisfy some institution's requirements.) In original research the researcher will surely pose many hypotheses informally at several points in his work, since almost every observation he makes will confirm, deny or modify a guess, a conjecture, speculation, or assumption in his own thinking. Later, in reporting on his work, he may indicate one or another hypothesis with which he was concerned, but it may not have been the one with which he began his inquiry. The automatic use of formally stated hypotheses, and of statements of "the problem" may make it easier to program action, but it will also limit the kinds of experience that he will tolerate and deal with. In original research there is less likely to be a conceptual closure to inquiry, for as the work of discovery continues and new kinds of data are conceptualized, new problems and hypotheses quite naturally will emerge. Consequently, far from putting a closure on his new experience the researcher will modify his problem and hypotheses—if indeed he had ever stated them explicitly—arrange to handle new ones simultaneously with the old, or do so in serial order. This is how the relation between the observer and the observed object is altered, and how it becomes possible for new questions to be asked and answered through research.

Concluding Note

Our discussion in this chapter has undoubtedly been all too abstract, though we believed it necessary to touch on a number of issues, both philosophic and practical, to have a proper basis for subsequent discussion. Perhaps now—before moving to chapters dealing with actual field operations—we require a brief, general statement that will lead into our description of what the field researcher does when he is in the field.

The observer of human events listens to how persons in given situations present to themselves and to others (including the naturalist) the "realities" and contexts of their lives. Meanwhile, he correlates what he himself sees with what he hears from these persons who stand in different relationships to each other and to the whole situation. The observer is then able to develop an abstract, logical, and empirically grounded representation of the observed situation. In and through his representation, the researcher is able to construct still other situational properties about social processes not otherwise apparent, but which relate directly to the one he is observing. His task requires distinctive and flexible strategies to maximize discovery in the situation—a situation special in many ways but particularly in that the observer is an outsider in an otherwise "inside world." He too becomes caught up in the situation he has set out to examine, and undoubtedly he knows that his presence changes the situation. He develops strategies for mitigating, accounting for, or otherwise taking advantage of the effects of his presence. Whatever strategy he uses will depend upon the whole situation.

What we are saying here, with respect to observations of actual situations, refers directly to what is known as the *field method*—a generic term for observing events in a natural situation. The activities of the naturalist in sociology and anthropology have distinct similarities to those of naturalists in zoology, archeology and geology. Sociologists and anthropolgists use this field method, but not all are humanists in the sense in which we have discussed "humanism." Many are mechanists insofar as they use functional, organic models for conceiving of human relations. Therefore, field method as such is not exclusive to the humanistic perspective. Also from the assumption we have made about man creating his own world, it follows that the naturalist as researcher will not, in advance, presuppose more than the barest rudiments of social order and social value. What he will do is to maximize the possibilities of discovering these as they are developed by people within the situation.

Also, we would make clear that the field method is not an exclusive method in the same sense, say, that experimentation is. Field method is more like an umbrella of activity beneath which any technique may be used for gaining the desired information, and for processes of thinking about this information. As part of field method, the researcher can examine historical documents and other secondary sources—since most situations which are studied have histories and these documents often make some aspects of the situation more understandable. (In a sense, reading documents is equivalent to making critical, careful observations of the situation through instruments devised by others.) Likewise, in field research one can survey a sample of a large population to obtain different kinds of leads on the situation which is also being examined up close. Case studies of persons, occupations, and other classes of person or events may be of help too. Though each technique has its own logic and can be used exclusively, there is no rule which forbids using a mixture of them in field work. Even experimentation of a sort can be worked into a field study, though usually this is done after an initial period of observation designed to learn how this situation normally would be. The field researcher is a pragmatist, all the more so because he is not constrained to articulate in advance a specific technique or specific problem.

Suggested Reading

A. A brief selection of readings bearing generally upon the field method of research and the logic of its operations.

BLUMER, HERBERT, *Symbolic Interactionism.* Englewood Cliffs, N.J.: Prentice-Hall, Inc., 1969.

A collection of articles on topics of importance to social psychology dealt with by a foremost symbolic interactionist. Chapter I brilliantly and succinctly lays out the essence of this perspective and indicates methodological implications that are important for field work.

BRUYN, SEVERYN, *The Human Perspective*. Englewood Cliffs, N.J.: Prentice-Hall, Inc., 1966.

An excellent general text on methodology which provides historical, philosophical, and sociological roots and rationale for field research into human social situations.

DENZIN, NORMAN K., "The Logic of Naturalistic Inquiry," in *Social Forces,* L, No. 2 (1971), 166–82.

Denzin develops the "position that naturalism is a logical outcome of the pragmatist, symbolic interactionist conception of sociology, man and society."

DEUTSCHER, IRWIN, "Words and Deeds: Social Science and Social Policy," in *Social Problems,* XIII, 233–54; also in William J. Filstead, *Qualitative Methodology: Firsthand Involvement with the Social World.* Chicago: Markham Publishing Co., 1970.

An article dealing with apparent discrepancies between what people say and what they do, and their implications for social research and social policy. Well worth reading and pondering.

DEWEY, JOHN, *Logic: The Theory of Inquiry*. New York: Holt, Rinehart and Winston, 1938.

The early chapters contain one of the clearest statements ever published on the relationship among problem, method, and technique.

GLASER, BARNEY G. and ANSELM STRAUSS, *The Discovery of Grounded Theory: Strategies for Qualitative Research.* Chicago: Aldine Publishing Co., 1967.

This book has been widely read as a justification for doing qualitative research, though it is much more than that. Chapters I, IX, and XI have, perhaps, the most bearing upon the foregoing pages.

MEAD, GEORGE HERBERT, *Mind, Self and Society*. Chicago: The University of Chicago Press, 1934.

An early and original source on the theoretical perspective taken here; well worth examining.

TINBERGEN, NIKO, *Curious Naturalists*. Garden City, N.Y.: Anchor Books, Doubleday & Co., The Natural History Library, 1958.

Expresses beautifully the attitude and some of the supporting philosophy of the naturalist. The student of social science should read, at least, the first and last chapters of the book, and ponder Tinbergen's view that extended field observations of natural events provide natural or unplanned experiments.

B. Books (mostly readings) on field research with emphases upon operations and researcher roles.

ADAMS, R. N. and J. J. PREISS (eds.), *Human Organization Research.* Homewood, Ill.: The Dorsey Press, 1960.

An "early" collection of articles (1940–1960) republished from *Human Organization* and its predecessor *Applied Anthropology.* The authors are from many fields and the collection reflects this diversity. Provided is an extensive bibliography particularly rich in anthropological materials of the era.

FILSTEAD, WILLIAM J., *Qualitative Methodology: Firsthand Involvement with the Social World.* Chicago: Markham Publishing Co., 1970.

A general and useful collection of articles covering such topics as field work roles, data collection, analysis, problems of validation and reliability, ethical issues, and the relations of qualitative data to social theory. Articles on field work are included. Filstead's introductory chapter is particularly pertinent.

JUNKER, BUFORD H., *Field Work: An Introduction to the Social Sciences.* Chicago: The University of Chicago Press, 1960.

This book consists of a stimulating introduction by Everett Hughes plus a running text containing extensive quotations and field notes from workers in the field, principally sociologists and anthropologists. The book is especially useful for illustrations of commentaries on field worker roles and adaptations. An extensive bibliography is provided covering major monographs.

McCALL, GEORGE J. and J. L. SIMMONS, *Issues in Participant Observation: A Text and Reader.* Reading, Mass.: Addison-Wesley Publishing Co., 1969.

In our judgment this is the best reader on field work. It is also, in part, a text, in which very pertinent issues in field work are raised. It has an extensive bibliography covering virtually all aspects of field work.

OLESEN, VIRGINIA, "Naturalism in Nursing Research: Participant Observation and Studies of Students," in Phyllis Verhonik, *Research in Nursing Based on Psychosocial Data* (forthcoming).

A succinct and excellent piece of writing on many aspects of field research; also, an impressive bibliography which should prove most helpful.

C. Books (mostly readings) by researchers describing their experiences in the field, although not all using "field techniques"; emphasis on researcher thought and decision in widely different contexts.

BOWEN, ELENORE SMITH, *Return to Laughter.* New York: Harper & Row, 1954.

A fascinating and candid account of what happened to a novitiate researcher during her first major field research experience.

GOLDE, PEGGY, *Women in the Field: Anthropological Experiences.* Chicago: Aldine Publishing Co., 1970.

A collection of revelations of the work and life in the field of women anthropologists. A reading of at least a few of these accounts is recommended for purposes of feeling and understanding what it must be like to study strange worlds.

HABENSTEIN, ROBERT W., *Pathways to Data: Field Methods for Studying Ongoing Social Organizations.* Chicago: Aldine Publishing Co., 1970.

An excellent and useful reader on actual research, covering problems and techniques used in studies of many different types of social organization and population. Most articles are written around problems of access, observation, and interviewing with important insights and suggestions on field research processes.

HAMMOND, PHILLIP, *Sociologists at Work*. New York: Basic Books, Inc., 1964.

A good collection of accounts—written in the first person—of eminent social scientists who tell how they did research and why they did it their way. Although participant observation as a method was not often utilized by these researchers, the reader will surely benefit from an examination of these accounts.

SPINDLER, GEORGE D. (ed.), *Being an Anthropologist: Fieldwork in Eleven Cultures*. New York: Holt, Rinehart and Winston, Inc., 1970.

A set of readings prepared by contemporary anthropologists on their work with exotic and not-so-exotic peoples. The book is particularly useful because it reveals highly personalized accounts of field work and of tactics employed according to the special requirements of diverse situations.

VIDICH, ARTHUR J., JOSEPH BENSMAN, and MAURICE R. STEIN, *Reflections on Community Studies*. New York: John Wiley & Sons, Inc., 1964.

Another important anthology (collection) of first-person accounts of operations and thought processes in research. Most authors used field work.

WAX, ROSALIE H., *Doing Fieldwork: Warnings and Advice*. Chicago: The University of Chicago Press, 1971.

A fine—even exciting—book on fieldwork; personalized accounts of field encounters with several distinct research projects; plenty of warnings and advice.

2

Strategy for Entering

Though the reader may have followed us to this point, and perchance developed some appreciation for the field researcher's philosophy and stance, and some of the logic underlying the work, he still has little information about how the researcher actually performs his many tasks. We turn now to discussing these according to the emergent, strategic requirements that broadly structure and guide the operations. The strategic requirements are virtually self-explanatory: once the researcher has his focus of interest, he must locate a site that contains people and social activity bearing upon that interest; then, he must enter the site, establish an identity and relations with the host, watch the people and their activity, listen to the symbolic sounds that will make meaningful much of what goes on there, record his experiences, convert these experiences into data, analyze them, and validate his new understanding. How he handles these general requirements constitute his tactics.

We begin our discussion of field operations with a model of a researcher who has only a general substantive interest, a somewhat more specific focus of attention (the equivalent of a research problem), and an eye on a site that he assumes is suitable for study. According to our earlier stated limitations, this researcher has no free access to the site. We deliberately place this "handicap" upon him to insure—for the benefit of the reader, as a novice—that we provide at least some considerations bearing upon "getting in" and "staying in." The latter is especially important, since naturalistic field research into human relations is accomplished principally *through* human relations, and they require some care to establish and maintain.

Casing and Approaching

We have already dealt at some length with "probleming," which otherwise might be regarded as the first stage in the research process. Now, the researcher attempts to locate his site. Though he may find one easily enough, he has little information about the people whom he would cast into the role of hosts, and he does not know whether they would appreciate his presence there. Hence, he "cases the joint" carefully—for three simple reasons: (1) to determine as precisely as possible whether this site does, in fact, meet his substantive requirements—a question of *suitability;* [1] (2) to "measure" some of its presenting properties (size, population, complexity, spatial scatter, etc.) against his own resources of time, mobility, skills, and whatever else it would take to do the job—a question of *feasibility;* and (3) to gather information about the place and people there in preparation for negotiating entry—a question of *suitable tactics.* This last point bears some elaboration.

The field researcher will wish to know in advance some of the general and specific characteristics of the people, so that when later he presents himself and his objectives, he will know at least whom to approach, and how. He needs information on the identities and power alignments of the principals at the site—what they do, what their immediate interests and concerns are, including some of the vocabulary with which these currently are being expressed. Of considerable tactical value would be some knowledge of the temporal work rhythms of the people there; for the researcher knows that his point of entry—as the start of a career of sorts—cuts across the careers of those he would study; he and his work might be acceptable at one moment but not another, and to one of the principal hosts but not to another. This may be as complicated as knowing about an ongoing struggle for leadership or as simple as knowing that a Tuesday is better than a Monday for beginning his negotiation. In this connection, some history of the site, whether of a service institution or social movement, would be of value, including its succession of key persons, objectives and ideologies—all this, sufficiently accurate, even if sketchy, so as later not to

---

[1] According to our model, we ignore the common experience of allowing an "interesting" site to determine one's substantive interests.

embarrass or surprise anyone, including the researcher. Thus, to know in advance of negotiation about the routines, social structure, crises, and the realities of factionalism is to be at considerable advantage in the negotiation that must follow.

The researcher can skillfully garner information from a variety of sources, and with reasonable "counting" and "discounting," learn enough to present himself advantageously to the right persons at the right time. He examines documents, if there are such: newspaper accounts, brochures, or institutional histories. He can turn to former or present associates of the group for informal conversation, or visit the site for a look-see. The researcher need not, at this point, tip his hand by identifying himself or his plans to anyone; but he may do so if, in his judgment, a trial balloon will provide both data and a test of receptivity. One cannot establish a rule here—much will depend upon the researcher's good judgment, timing, and tact.

The same may be said for how the researcher later will make the first more or less formal contact. This not only involves judgment, timing, and tact, but also some skill at approach and engagement as necessary processes for entering new social relations. The researcher adopts tactics which are comfortable for him: some researchers use the phone easily; some prefer writing first, and then following up with a visit. Or, it may be convenient as well as comfortable to have some member or friend of the group make the initial introduction. Any of these modes, or even a sequence of all of them, may adequately meet the requirements of approach and engagement. But particular caution must be exercised in the use of third parties: the "friend" may turn out to be somebody's enemy. After all, organizational life does not require love and consensus among the membership. Finally, the researcher will "work the hierarchy" if one is discernible. When he enters with the permission of the "chief" host-to-be, or one of his "cabinet," he will later be better able to negotiate entry into the farthest reaches of the organization. To do otherwise is to invite angry challenge at a later point, and ejection from the site. Even if the chief is not in general favor, all persons in the organization will understand that the researcher could not otherwise have gained authorization. Once authorization is gained, the researcher symbolically disengages himself from the leadership in order to establish his independence.

Our own experiences with entering sites for purposes of study are highly varied. One illustration here will highlight some of the aforementioned remarks. Both of the authors are members of the faculty of a university school of nursing on a medical campus and have frequently entered a ward of the training hospital via the nursing service. One of us tried the same tactic to enter a nearby county hospital which also had a training and service affiliation with the university. Indeed, the nursing service of this hospital assumed it had the authority to facilitate entry: after all, the researcher did plan to observe and speak with nurses. Yet, the clinical chief denied this authorization, and requested that the researcher remove himself from the premises until such time as he obtained permission from the chief county medical officer. He did so and subsequently returned to the county hospital, but even then had so aroused the suspicion and anger of the local chief that he was kept waiting for several weeks before local entrée was granted. Subsequently, the researcher learned that he had been "punished" for his transgression: the local chief "ran a tight ship," regarded the county chief with contempt, and had never made such a request before of anyone who asked *his* permission for entrée. This series of events might never have happened had the researcher made a simple inquiry among any number of knowledgeable people about the local chief and his relation to *his* hospital.

Under special circumstances the researcher needs to make several entries, each to a different site. His multiple entries may derive from the purposes of the research itself. Thus, he must do field work at several different hospitals, because he wishes to make a comparative analysis either of the hospitals themselves or of comparable medical wards found in them. His work of entrée certainly is not finished after he has gotten permission to do research at only one site. Multiple entries may also be required by the character of the phenomenon that he wishes to study: a geographically scattered or amorphous social movement may necessitate virtually separate entries at each specific locale. At each site the researcher must establish his credibility and begin to enter into relationships useful for his research purposes.

Entering into Relationships

Despite considerable writing about field work, relatively little information is available specifically on the problem of entrée and on tactics used to effect it. The paucity of information is understandable, since field researchers characteristically become preoccupied with data that begin to flow in very quickly after having gained entrée. Then the drama and importance of early researcher-host encounters may no longer command attention, so that by the time the researcher is preparing his work for publication, he is not particularly interested in recounting the steps he took to get into the study site, even when describing his method of work, unless entrée was particularly difficult or unusual.

Yet, the matters of entrée and of establishing amicable relations are of such great importance that we need at least to review the more salient considerations that any field researcher must bear in mind. Considering that people's privacies are to be "invaded," that commitments to their work and even their very identity are likely to be called into question, it does not take much imagination to realize how tactical error, blunder, or social crudity can complicate an otherwise worthy project—not to mention the cost to the researcher of having to find a new site or to abandon a study altogether. In a mutually voluntary and negotiated entrée, the host holds options not only to prevent entrée but to terminate relations with the researcher at almost any stage thereafter. This suggests that how one gets in and manages to stay in will shape, if not determine, what one gets out of the site and its host.

Furthermore, it suggests that entrée is a *continuous* process of establishing and developing relationships, not alone with a chief host but with a variety of less powerful persons. In relatively complex sites, particularly those with multiple leadership and jurisdictions, there are many doorways that must be negotiated; successful negotiation through the front door is not always sufficient to open other doors, though at first it may appear to do just that. In many situations, the chief host may not himself have the kind of access to his own sub-jurisdictions that a good field researcher requires; he may be hated or feared. Often, interior organizational lines lead to districts guarded by lesser chiefs who also exercise options—if not to bar physical access, then to withhold a necessary level of cooperation. Some institutions and social movements have stronger local barons than emperors; therefore, the researcher endeavors to negotiate his own way through every door. Wisdom dictates that the approach to people anywhere in the hierarchy, and negotiation with them, will not be unlike the initial one at the "front door." This includes "casing" the sub-site ahead of time —a task rendered somewhat easier than the original grande entrée, since not only will he pick up cues about sub-sites from his initial quick visit there but from conversations elsewhere that touch on particular sub-sites; if need be, he can ask judicious questions about the one he is about to visit ("tell me a little about what goes on at . . .").

Some time ago, after having negotiated entry into a state hospital which was organized around both a "chronic service" and "treatment services," we and other colleagues tactically chose to study the chronic wards first. Some evidence and much thought about the relations between these divisions—and how each might view us—led to this decision. We had learned that visitors rarely came to the "back wards" to study them; they came only to "investigate"; and that the reverse was more probably true for the treatment services. Indeed, when both were visited, it was usually the latter first, and the former second. Considering that to the clinically oriented people the chronic wards would be seen as second best, if not abominable, and that the personnel there would always sense the invidiousness of any such comparison, we entered the chronic section first and represented ourselves as wanting to study the hospital—them! They were delighted and flattered.

Thus, the experienced researcher recognizes that entering relatively complex human organizations is a process in which he will be engaged long after "permission" to enter has been granted. The continuity is assured on two counts: first, to the extent that anyone in the organization has autonomy and some options on cooperation, *each person,* theoretically, must be negotiated with; second, relationships that are initially established naturally do change—and not always for the better. After all, the researcher will be in the field for weeks or months; he will change as he learns more about the people and their work. His study will lead him to unanticipated perspectives and unanticipated places; therefore his actions—and identity—will also change and probably impel frequent reaffirmations of his person and purposes. On some sub-sites there may be some change of personnel, even of the chief authority there, so new exploration of purpose and renegotiation must occur. Likewise, over time, the work of the many hosts will be different—or appear so—and the hosts will be variously embarrassed, outraged, or pleased with their own performance under scrutiny. Finally, the researcher will find that his relations with some hosts will be so tangential to his developing objectives, and his visits with them so intermittent, that he will find it necessary again and again to identify himself—and probably to apologize for not observing or listening to them as much as to others. Often, the very persons who at first seek to avoid the observer's eye or ear are the ones who later feel insulted for his not valuing their persons and work.

The underlying message here is that good human relations in field research require considerable attention and intelligent regulation. They do not guarantee good results but are prerequisite to gaining and maintaining entrée ultimately into a world and sub-worlds of meaning—of nuance in thought and of subtle variations in human conduct. The field researcher needs to create situations which invite visibility and disclosure for others; otherwise, he is left to construct his sociology out of clichés, platitudes, literal performance, plus whatever meanings he can derive.

Presenting Self and Study

Having sized up the site and found it suitable, the researcher can prepare a statement for the host about himself and his work. The statement identifies him, his sponsor or organizational affiliation, his study objectives, and his method of work. Though the statement need not be in writing, a document for limited distribution will prove most helpful, particularly where large numbers of persons are institutionally organized and spatially scattered. Certainly, a written statement may have no importance as a tactic for entering an amorphous social movement or an aggregate distinguished only for its adherence to a fad. However, the principle of preparation is of considerable importance—even for the experienced researcher whose current objectives may be vague or abstract to others or even to himself. By preparing to tell others what he is up to, or intends to do, the researcher is telling himself as well—clarifying his "problem" and purposes, and mentally ordering at least his initial procedures. While he may be quite tolerant of his own vagueness, the hosts-to-be may not. One of them, at least, may have had a course in research methodology!

It is important for the researcher to get his "story line" straight; he will probably have to repeat it time and again. There is another reason for a document, particularly when researching in institutions: it is not uncommon that the principal host is unable easily to communicate to others the pertinent information on the researcher—even the name of the researcher. A document helps him represent the researcher to others, particularly his intentions, without an excess of distortion. It will also save the chief time and work. Copies of the document sent along to others in the organization will not only uniformly inform key persons but will forewarn them, and thereby prevent surprise and embarrassment—surprise from encounter without adequate preparation and embarrassment from later forgetting the stranger's identity, purposes, and even authorization. The researcher cannot depend upon routine channels of institutional communication to insure clarity, consistency of communication, and clearance into sub-jurisdictions.

The statement itself should be brief and carefully worded so that all classes of person at the site will be able to understand it. It should not be very detailed (a page or two) because the field researcher does not want to make a firm commitment to a problem or too narrow a focus. In addition to proffering the facts of his identification, the statement should assure all hosts of confidentiality and very explicitly separate the researcher from any given source of power within or outside the group—the principal chief or chiefs, as well as police and mass media. It clearly shows the researcher's respect for integrity of the members and their work. Also, the statement should indicate approximately how long, with their permission, the study will go on and how much or how little work will be demanded of them. If the researcher is to get permission at all, the hosts will be delighted that he will "stay with it" for a long or appreciable amount of time, and that he asks for virtually nothing but access to persons, places, and harmless existing documents.

Since the researcher can expect the host to request some feedback or "service," he will wisely indicate in the statement that in due time he will have some interesting and useful "observations" to offer; he is not a "hit-and-run" researcher. Moreover, if publication is one of the purposes of the research, the researcher will assure the host of anonymity when required and whenever possible. Finally, in writing or when presenting his statement, the researcher should play down any expertise or profound knowledge he may have on the subject of which the hosts may claim to be expert: the researcher is and should act the learner, indicating no inclination to evaluate the host's activities. Although presumably all this can be communicated verbally, a document which succinctly says as much saves the host's and researcher's time, gives a defense against considerable misunderstanding, and provides a particularly good excuse for persons at the site later to engage with the researcher comfortably. While such a formal statement by no means guarantees entrée, it goes a long way towards answering the probable questions raised by anyone who hosts research. It has, after all, the advantage of preparation, and sets a good stage for negotiation.

Here is an example of an entrée letter actually sent:

Dear Dr. _____:

You will recall we chatted briefly at the meeting of the _____.
I indicated, then, my interest in a study of changes in psychiatric organization and operations as the county system evolves from that of a centralized, professionally controlled enterprise to that of a dispersed community enterprise. I would want to discover the kinds of structural problems that may develop in this transition and, particularly, the ways these problems are defined and managed. Naturally, I hope that you will find such a study to be both interesting to you and advantageous as you and your staff ponder and deal with some of the very same problems.

In so brief a note, it is not possible to provide greater detail on the study objectives, although I would be most pleased to discuss these further with you. Here, however, I wish to assure you that I have no hidden agenda, for example, such as an effort to evaluate the work of your group; also to assure you that any future publication which may result from this study will fully generalize findings and mask the identities of persons and organization for everyone's protection.

With your permission—and that of your co-professionals—I would spend a few months observing and listening for matters related to the transition. This means making it possible for me to gain access to staff meetings and other activities which might shed some light on specific events—access at my own discretion, although not without due regard to personal (staff or patient) and clinical requirements for privacy. Except for brief interviews (really conversations) I will not "make work" or otherwise complicate the efforts of your staff.

At later stages in the study, I will surely find one or another occasion to talk with the staff about some of my developing ideas; and surely at the conclusion of the study, I would be prepared to report to all the staff on findings pertinent to its interests. In this way, I hope my work would be of some value, and reciprocate your cooperation in the research project.

I will be phoning you within a few days, and would be happy to visit with you at any time thereafter for any matters you may wish to discuss with me.

Sincerely,

Entering Informal Movements

When entrée into a relatively amorphous movement is sought, a somewhat different tactical plan is necessary. Of course, the strategy is the same: to engage the host and to find acceptance for the study. But an emergent movement may have no central or formal leadership, and no central locus of operations. Indeed, persons in the movement may not themselves know "who belongs," or how many others identify (and in what ways) with the movement. The kind of movement itself will suggest some of the tactics. Thus, movements which seek widespread support and membership may be quite easy to enter for membership or for study, whereas a militant movement, or one which purports to represent the interests of some special class of people—by age, ethnicity, occupation, or other—may prove more difficult to break into, particularly when the person of the researcher is visibly alien to the social category most represented.

Yet, assuming it is at all possible to enter, the researcher can begin to gather his data even as he cases the movement. If, indeed, the movement has few institutional properties—particularly no established or central leadership—the field researcher must set about to discover by whom, and from where, organization is being developed. Since the movement probably will have visible even if scattered signs of existence, the researcher seeks out locations where members or advocates assemble. With no one to help lead him in, the researcher may first have to seek out public gathering places. There he informally engages any advocate in conversation and begins the development of successive bits of data, going on to many other advocates who, in turn, become informants. At this stage, the data he seeks most are those which locate places and persons of significance to the movement, although in order to get such information, he may find it necessary to listen at length to ideological assertion. But all this provides data, too, and eventually, the researcher will hear of an emergent leadership (central, peripheral, or scattered) somewhere and will make his way towards it. Then, he may go through the motions of identifying himself and his interests and request entrée, even though it may already have substantially been achieved.

In contrast to the initial contact with institutional leadership, the researcher need not quickly make a statement of personal identification or objectives. He can elect to wait until it is necessary or advantageous to do so. Generally, the more he knows about the movement in advance, and the more comfortable he is in its environs, the more likely that the time for disclosure is his own option. But when his observations lack meaning because of his own failure to understand what he sees and hears, he can save himself much time and trouble by identifying himself early, thereby bringing others quickly to the point of articulating the substance of their world. Though the researcher can elect to remain incognito for programmatic reasons, the more alien he appears and the more "unnatural" his behavior, the more quickly is his disclosure required. Certainly when the time comes for him to ask certain questions—and in a special way—he will reveal himself and his objectives; for not to do so at the right time—except in the most benign social movements—is to court embarrassment and suspicion of his motives.

Preparing for Negotiation

What can be said about preparing for negotiation with the host? To some extent the researcher has already set a good stage for it: he has promised confidentiality, respect, objectivity, and implicitly promised to behave well, as a guest, in the house of a host. Now, what can be anticipated as a reception to all this? The reception can go a number of ways, because hosts have their own comprehensions of both the requirements of their organizations and the meanings of social research. The researcher can anticipate some of what may occur through effective "casing." However, he must be prepared for a range of probable responses to his request for entrée: delight with the interest shown by an outsider, fear of publicity or exposé, hope of obtaining free information or consultation, annoyance, or general disinterest. Also, hosts may be so "sophisticated" in research as to respect only their own conception of proper problem and appropriate method, or so "ignorant" of research as to be unable even to ask appropriate questions about its conduct and purposes. Other, more particular, responses may emerge: for example, the hosts may not be satisfied with the status of the researcher ("only a student"), may hold a low opinion of the researcher's affiliation or sponsoring organization (Gazebo College), or may regard the focus of study as irrelevant. Yet, short of outright rejection (in contrast to disinterest or fear) on whatever grounds, any particular counter by the host will provide opportunities for the negotiation. Shortly, we shall deal with some of the ways the researcher can bargain for acceptance.

How a host handles the initial encounter depends, in part, upon how he comprehends social research. The experienced field researcher expects and has learned to contend with the highly probable view by the host that research into human social organization is functional and evaluative—even clinical—in orientation and objectives. The host may believe it is a kind of "systems analysis." *Functionalism* in sociology has repeatedly re-inforced the practical man's notion that social scientists are concerned mainly with the proper assignment and exercise of social roles, the rationali-zation or effectiveness of organization, and the measurement of activity in the context of declared goals. This probable view has important implica-tions for entry negotiations, for it may mean the host happily anticipates, by way of research, a search for sources of conflict and malfunction, or the measurement of morale, and the like. If so, the researcher does not go out of his way to deny these concerns, even if he is not at all interested in them; later they may come in handy as negotiating counters. Besides, to deny interest in them altogether, unless really necessary, is to challenge the host's conception of what the social scientist is and what he does and this may be too upsetting. But, however the hosts interpret the researcher's objectives and his reasons for doing research, they are unlikely to vary much in their expectations that he will accept the people there, and their work, at face value; that is, that they are authentic and their activity is good and valid. They may allow the researcher ultimately to question the *efficiency* of their work, and even its efficacy, but are not likely to accept much question of its validity or ultimate value. Hence, the researcher is careful never to project cynicism about the hosts and their activities.

Finally, the researcher understands that the hosts may not appreciate his need for conceptual distance or transcendence and his needs to keep his own counsel and serve his own interests first and foremost. This is par-ticularly so at sites where commitment and service are regarded as universal properties of work there. This is not an insurmountable problem, however, though it can prove most troublesome. How the researcher handles this problem and others like it is the next topic.

Negotiation in the Context
of Reciprocity

The researcher's request for entrée may mark the beginning of negotiation between the parties. The negotiation may be quite subtle, even implicit, or take the form of hard bargaining. In either case, this negotiation is not between contending parties, in which each seeks to exact something from the other without giving anything in return; this one seeks to develop relations in the context of reciprocity. Assuming entry is to be granted or gained at all, each party's primary concern is freedom of action and the integrity of his position. For the researcher, this means his own relative freedom to move about, to look and listen—also, to think in his own terms, and to communicate his thoughts to his own intellectual community. For the host, it means freedom for him and his group to pursue their work unencumbered and unafraid. This is why the researcher unequivocally assures the host of confidentiality and anonymity. On his own part, the researcher will make explicit, if necessary, his own requirements.

But what if—despite good will—the hosts define the research requirements differently, or are so fearful of disclosure that they attempt to bargain away the requirements? Though the researcher may hope his own independence and freedom are not subject to bargaining, he cannot expect that his hosts will always fully understand and appreciate this point. He makes his own decisions concerning what he will and will not bargain. Before we discuss the actual transaction, we would make a single, important point: *any restrictions initially accepted by the researcher should be regarded as renegotiable at later, more propitious times.* Once initial entry is made, new relations can be skillfully developed so that in time virtually complete (or at least much more) freedom is gained. The hosts may simply require a period of testing to insure that the researcher's objectives are indeed consistent with their own. Then a colleagueship of sorts may develop, which will open doors to even the most secret and sacred of rites and of thoughts.

Clearly, the researcher will not bargain on his own requirement for independence; he is neither a captive nor a partisan of any person or group. He shares his findings and his understandings with any or all, or with no one. This rule is both ethically and tactically correct. Then, on what will the researcher bargain—again, at least initially? He will bargain some of his *freedom of access.* Of course, he alone can judge how much he can bargain away and still perform tasks he has set for himself. Does he need to see all the documents, interview everyone, observe anywhere at any time? Aside from simply arguing the necessity for complete access, or of quickly succumbing to many restrictions, perhaps out of fear of being refused entrée altogether, the researcher avoids specific and binding agreements at this time. By tactically agreeing not to invade sensitive areas without permission, *at the time access is actually deemed necessary,* he may succeed in distributing the responsibility for granting it to many persons, thereby gaining for himself both time and multiple opportunities for bargaining at the point of necessity. In early negotiations, the researcher will have gained much intelligence on what are considered sensitive areas, and will time his observations there for relatively later penetration. A final word on access: it relates to freedom of movement and not necessarily to the integrity of the research or the researcher; therefore, the researcher does not define that freedom in vital, personal terms.

What of bagaining about problem or foci of interests? At best, the hosts want little more than a sympathetic ear; at worst, they suggest problems for research of interest or importance to themselves. At the outset—even earlier, when casing the site—the researcher thinks not only about what the site may offer him, but also what its hosts may demand or need. Indeed, he might well have asked himself, at some early time, why any host should want to put up with him at all. With this attitude and with some ingenuity, the researcher is in an excellent position to bargain around mutual interests. He does have some distinct advantages, principally that his theoretical perspective and interests, if at all relevant to human group experience, can be conceptually translated into words of concrete relevance to the hosts. What institutional or group leaders are not interested in problems of control, communication, coordination? What leaders of social movements are not interested in learning the extent of their appeal, even within their following, or not seriously concerned with the extent to which their ideology is comprehended? A skilled researcher will examine his own objectives carefully and prepare himself, well in advance, to make the translation and then, crudely put, to "sell" it.

If this mainly persuasive tactic strikes no positive chord in the host, then the researcher may well consider incorporating into his work some of what the host suggests. He himself will have to gauge the extent to which the "suggestion" is a condition for his entrée. Even if it is, the suggested problem can be transformed to suit both theoretical and practical interests. Actually, the researcher will not be too surprised to discover, weeks later, that the host has all but forgotten his own suggestion, or is no longer pressing for specific findings. Taking still another perspective, it is quite possible that a particular host is sophisticated enough to provide not only a significant focus or problem but excellent clues as to how to get the data. Assuming, as we have, that the researcher brought with him neither firm design nor an exact or immutable problem, he may well accept some part of the host's request, providing it is consistent with his own general objectives and requirements: a small price to pay for entry, and perhaps even of great value.

A more difficult, but negotiable, issue is presented by a host who requests or insists upon the researcher's performing some work in addition to the research, for example, teaching about or evaluating some aspect of the collective life he is studying. The researcher can refuse, but even here, a refusal need not be unequivocal. In accord with our model of field research, the investigator is a guest and will leave a gift in the form of abstracted information that is of value to the host. The researcher may need only to make slight alterations in its presentation to satisfy the host. He does not thereby compromise his roles as researcher if he agrees to speak with a representative group of hosts about some of his observations and thoughts—at an appropriate time. With some skill he may even be able to turn his offering into a seminar and get further data—more actually than he gives. Better still, he may test the validity of some of his emerging propositions. Thus, in the negotiations, the researcher himself may establish the form of his contribution.

One of us recalls—with humor but only in retrospect—of a research training project, wherein the author, one other faculty colleague, and two students traveled from the west coast to the Fort Logan Mental Health Center in Colorado for a five-week field exercise. We had agreed, for the privilege of entrée, to present a final verbal report to all the hosts. Our initial plan was to halt our observations a day or so before report time and "casually" prepare a brief verbal statement. Word of this agreement between chief host and the research group spread quickly throughout the center. Soon personnel were—from the very first day—greeting us with: "We can't wait until we get your report." So incessant did this cry become that the students in the research group became too anxious to do their work well. This situation was exacerbated when personnel on several of the wards exacted promises from the students of special reports on themselves exclusive of the others. Soon, it appeared, the team was working for the center and not for itself. The reader can well imagine how late into each night we worked and how furiously we analyzed our data. Yet, we did not lose sight of our objectives. The individual reports prepared collectively by the students and faculty provided excellent opportunity for feedback of theoretical propositions gained through analysis, and this, in turn, figured prominently in the subsequent report to the entire group of hosts. A "moral" may be drawn from this illustration: that negotiation may take on the character of a career, often with no predictable bench marks or end point; also that tacit side agreements can be made without knowing in advance their implications, or even without fully realizing that one has made them.

Finally, there is the matter of methodology as an item of negotiation. Generally, the field researcher is concerned with qualitative data, and seeks to apply his own special mode of analysis to them. How he organizes and experiences them expresses his own identity as an observer and social analyst. On this he cannot compromise, though he can tactically offer to work some data differently—but only additionally, *not* instead of how he must finally deal with them. Other aspects of methodology can be negotiated which are more peripheral to research identity than the mode of analysis: operations related to timing and sequence of observation, interview technique, physical vantage points for observing, and even note-taking while observing. Concerning these, the researcher negotiates and later renegotiates as he moves about from locale to locale within the site and from person to person. Most often his success depends simply on taking into account the comfort and convenience of a particular host or subgroup. In the next chapter we shall be concerned with these and other tactics.

Suggested Reading

A. Some articles of value to aspiring field researchers bearing in some part upon establishing workable arrangements with hosts.

BECK, BERNARD, "Cooking Welfare Stew," in Robert W. Habenstein, *Pathways to Data: Field Methods for Studying Ongoing Social Organizations.* Chicago: Aldine Publishing Co., 1970.

An article covering lightly—but with useful advice—important aspects of field research. Emphases on entering and establishing relations.

DEAN, JOHN P., ROBERT L. EICHORN, and LOIS R. DEAN, "Observation and Interviewing," in John T. Doby (ed.), *An Introduction to Social Research* (2nd ed.), pp. 274–304. Des Moines, Iowa: Meredith Corporation, 1967.

A good discussion of principles leading to effective relations between researcher and host; especially pp. 281–83.

KAHN, ROBERT, and FLOYD MANN, "Developing Research Partnerships," *Journal of Social Issues,* VIII, No. 3, 4–10; also in McCall-Simmons, *Issues in Participant Observation: A Text and Reader.* Reading, Mass.: Addison-Wesley Publishing Co., 1969.

A discussion of multiple entry into organizations that have multiple authority structures and factions.

RICHARDSON, STEPHEN A., "A Framework for Reporting Field-Relations Experiences," in R. N. Adams and J. J. Preiss, *Human Organization Research,* pp. 124–39. Homewood, Ill.: The Dorsey Press, 1960.

A brief but very clear discussion of problems (and suggestions) bearing upon field researcher relations with the host, including entering and the later processes of work with the host.

WAX, ROSALIE, "Reciprocity in Field Work," in Adams and Preiss, *Human Organization Research,* pp. 90–98.

A classic article on reciprocity which provides sage advice on the processes of engaging the host and of holding his interest. It provides insight into the informant's motivation to cooperate.

————, "Twelve Years Later: An Analysis of Field Experiences," in Adams and Preiss, *Human Organization Research,* pp. 166–78.

A personalized and informative account of field work as a crucible in the making of a field researcher. A vivid example of how the role of the researcher is conditioned by relations with multiple hosts.

3

Strategy for Getting Organized

Mapping

The researcher has now gained formal entry, though he has come only through the front door. Armed with a measure of authority, he can move about the site with relative freedom. Now, also, he can attend to gathering data systematically—but quite possibly he does not yet have a workable and reliable perspective on the whole of his field; not even the more obvious, presenting properties are substantially known to him. What he requires is a working conception of the relevant dimensions of the site, including its outer boundaries and inner locales; [1] also, the classes of things, persons, and events which inhabit these locales. For all this, he requires a number of "maps": social, spatial, and temporal. In institutional research, such formal maps are usually available as tables of organization, schedules of routines and special meetings, and drawings of street and building plans. These maps are useful as aids to orientation in the early stages of research. They are data also: they indicate, in special form,

[1] A search for boundaries—outer or inner—may prove elusive, for relationships and functions flow into and out of most social units. Yet the researcher will have to set some limits for very practical reasons. He will do so after he has established his main foci of interest.

some of the reality that the hosts present to themselves and others. In the study of social movements, however, such maps are rare and probably not very reliable because of the more ephemeral nature of members and activities, and their temporal-spatial loci. Entrée may have been permitted in the expectation that the researcher himself will eventually provide the leadership with some reliable maps. In any event, how does the researcher provide himself with a set of maps on which he can depend?

He undertakes a mapping operation, moving among the various locales he knows of, listening for evidence of still others, and visiting most or all of these. This is a tour of limited discovery—a first reliable and extensive (not intensive) look at the things, persons, and activities that constitute the site. An operation of this sort is not mandatory, but if the researcher is to be systematic, he needs a sense of population or universe. Besides, given the complexity of the task before him, what better way is there for establishing the properties to be observed and priorities for dealing with them? In studying institutional phenomena of such complexity—where the parameters of the object exist in outline—this procedure is particularly economical of time and energy. When studying a movement, which has few or no clear lines, the universe may well be the last item discovered; mapping would then be indistinguishable from substantive data gathering, and not be at all a preliminary stage.

A number of tactical moves can help facilitate the mapping operation. The researcher can, of course, perform the task himself; but it is helpful to have the services of an informant or guide—a "man Friday"—to escort and inform him, and introduce him to many persons whom he will later wish to observe and speak with at greater length. A request that the leadership provide such a person offers two tactical advantages: the researcher gets the help he needs, and the leadership is assured that the guest will get to see the "right" things and people—and also be kept out of trouble. The researcher should suggest that the guide be a person of somewhat lesser rank and an "old-timer." Such a person is part of the history as well as the structure of the organization, and as he escorts the guest can indicate important elements of social process, particularly of social and ideological succession. He can introduce the researcher to people whom he knows, giving names, ranks, and relationships. In addition to or instead of a single guide, the researcher can establish the same relationship with certain individuals at the several sub-sites: "old-timers" and secretaries know a great deal about people and places and can be excellent informants; also, they wield special powers. However the mapping tour is arranged—with or without a guide—it is important that the researcher signal his arrival at locations in advance to avoid surprise and embarrassment. He can do this by phone, or have someone call ahead for him, thereby providing a social bridge from one key person and locale to the next.

Mapping serves a number of important research interests: methodological, interactional, and substantive. Of these, the most important is the first mentioned; for shortly the researcher will need to know what to watch and with whom to converse—where, when, how much—and in what order. Hence, in mapping the researcher attends particularly to demographic data. For his "social map," he records numbers and varieties of persons, their hierarchical arrangement, divisions of labor, and other facts pertinent to his own operational decisions. For the same reason the researcher constructs his "spatial map," locating persons, equipment, and specialized centers of work and control. He also notes the corridors along which pass people, goods, and services. His "temporal map" will contain data bearing upon the ebb and flow of people, goods, services and communications. He looks for and asks about schedules which tell of hourly, daily, and weekly rhythms of work and play; also, he locates, in time, the special assemblies, rituals, and routines that characterize the locations. After he does this, he is in an excellent position to adjust his own time and other resources to the research task—or even alter the task, since even a quick "look-see" may uncover properties that alter his perception of the magnitude or complexity of the site and therefore alter the scope and direction of his research. For example, very early in our study of a private psychiatric hospital we found it necessary to look beyond the hospital in order to explain its workings. We discovered that the psychiatrists and residents were intricately associated with outside professional organizations and that these associations significantly shaped their day-to-day operations and professional commitment to the hospital itself.

Visits to the many locations lead the researcher to people who are variously delighted or annoyed with his presence, hungry for recognition, eager for audience, or embarrassed by some immediate state of affairs which would be threatened by exposure. The researcher senses these postures and feelings; he sizes them up for the next tactical stage in his research, for unless he requires starting his systematic observation in one locale rather than another, he might as well take advantage of the varieties of reception given him. He might as well, also, temporarily avoid those locales which make him particularly uncomfortable or anxious by virtue either of the work done there or of the kind of people who work there—or both. It makes sense, then, to begin systematic observation where he is most welcome and feels least anxious. Thereby he both spares those at the site undue anxiety over his presence and gives other sites time to prepare a welcome at some later date. Besides, those who would welcome him now are likely to be more eager to teach and inform him, and this is precisely what he seeks. The skilled observer is not concerned with the bias implicit in the differences in receptivity at locales; as he proceeds, he learns what and what not to discount.

In the same way, the experienced field observer will learn how to deal with the variety of persons who very willingly or insistently cast themselves into helping roles as "research assistant," "confidant," "tipster," "friend" (or enemy) of the establishment. As enthusiasts, apologists, ideologues, or disgruntled detractors of the organization or movement, these persons provide many bits of very useful information. Their "biases" are no less data than that offered by the more "objective" members of organization. In fact, they may alert the observer to matters that probably he would not discover until weeks later. Hence, these persons also must be kept in mind for later work—not only for the help they offer but for the problems they pose, if they turn out to be pests.

Additionally, the mapping tour alerts persons in the many areas or jurisdictions to the presence of the researchers. Key persons may not have been properly informed (or informed at all) of the study, by the leadership or others. Moreover, these persons at the sub-sites must be brought to concur with the earlier granting of entrée by others, or brought to terms with it in a manner that is advantageous to the research. By presenting himself informally, for a brief visit, the researcher achieves some tactical advantages: he is in a position to inform people of the nature of his study, give them a chance to look him over, and allow them to "test" his stated interests as these might affect them. At this time, the researcher seemingly comes to meet people, and not to "work." Actually he is always working, but the thrust of his first visit is a casual one of socially natural introductions and mutual examination. In some respects, the visit "ennobles" the people, constituting an act of some symbolic importance to many sub-groupings who—particularly in the basements and odd corners of an organization—may feel tangential to central operations.

Of course, the mapping operation provides the researcher with substantive data, even though he may have attended to them mainly for their operational or interactional value. Some experiences are quickly recorded as *methodological notes,* some as *theoretical* (or *inferential*) *notes,* and some as *observation notes.* (See the chapter on strategy for recording.) At this stage of operations the researcher subordinates somewhat his substantive experiences to methodological ones, not only to provide himself with material that will help him plan his next stages, but also to avoid being "flooded" by a mass of new, exciting, and highly undifferentiated happenings. Novices waste much time and energy, and often become confused, when they try to attend to and record everything that they are experiencing; later they spend days wondering why they had done so. The experienced observer is not overly concerned about "missing" things; most of what occurs will happen again and again. If a specific event does not get repeated, another which points to the same underlying pattern of occurrences very likely will. Besides, we are dealing with an ongoing process, and the special or untoward event which happened the day before the research began is theoretically no more important than the one which happens during the research. Any field researcher will recognize the plaint: "You should have been here last week (month, year)!" He will only shrug his shoulders regretfully and ask, "Tell me about it. What happened then?" In any event, all recorded happenings are convertible to a variety of purposes; thus, the record of the name and status of a person, used to develop a social map for methodological purposes, is also a note pertaining to substantive purposes.

With some skill in observing, and through careful listening (and the right kinds of questioning), the researcher assembles the data pertinent to his maps. The information garnered to date from the "casing," the negotiation with the leadership, from informants and visits, constitutes not only mapping information but also initial data. Almost immediately the researcher can begin his analysis; he need not wait until "all" or "much" of the data are in to do his thinking. This is not, after all, a final analysis; it is only the beginning.

By now, he has a considerable amount of data, and depending upon his experience with similar phenomena he can begin to coordinate some facts and inferences, and develop some cogent propositions along with plans for checking them out. Propositional statements, hypotheses, or hunches about processes or structural properties may be little more than simple declarative sentences, but they can be linked to each other and to the starting framework of concepts about organization, communciation, control, socialization, and so on. Surely, many a historic decision affecting organizational policy is made with less care and in less time; but our researcher has a different kind of job to do. His understanding of the whole is still a bit shaky; it lacks validation if not plausibility, since at this point it is based as much upon his own past experience as upon his present ones.

Selective Sampling

Our field researcher now is in position to conduct selective observations at selected sub-sites. His mapping tour (or tours) has provided him with sets of population or universes—of people, places, events, and any other categories determined to be of some importance. He cannot hope to observe everything, since "everything"—even for a large research team—is only a theoretical possibility, particularly for such complex phenomena as we are dealing with here. Hence, selective sampling is a practical necessity and is theoretically mandatory; it is shaped by the time the researcher has available to him, by his framework, by his starting and developing interests, and by any restrictions placed upon his observation by his hosts.

Considering the stage of the research, and all that has happened to the researcher by way of experience, he may elect to step back—even leave the field for hours or days—to recoup his strength, to sort out what he has learned, and to decide more precisely upon his next sequence of operations. His strategy for the next stage is to move from one selected sub-site to another and sample at each site various "dimensions": time, space, people and events. Although his samples may appear to be numerically inadequate, it should be kept in mind that there is an "overlap" or intersection of these dimensions at all times. Thus, when the researcher samples persons, encounters with them will occur at a given time or over a span of time, at a place, in and around certain events. Even small samples of each dimension yield considerable "mileage" in the others.

Organizing time

First, a brief word about the sampling of time. The researcher now has a general idea about the temporal activities of the various people at the site. He knows something of the routine, and not so routine, rhythms of the place. Of course, 24 hours per day is a theoretical limit. Whether the organization is a hospital, factory or a police system, he must discover what occurs, say, at 2:00 A.M., just as he must at any other hour. In other organizations or perhaps in a social movement, people do not work around the clock either by shifts or any other way, and this fact will have to be taken into account; still, the researcher may discover later that, despite a presumed eight-hour work pattern, certain persons in almost every social organization may meet regularly in "off hours" to work, plan, or simply fashion ideologies through informal conversation. Then he will have to make his own plans accordingly.

Time can be broken into hours and sampled directly, or sampled through events and activities including routines. Thus, if meetings are held at 9:00 A.M., the researcher covers *both* time and activity. If the researcher elects to observe work around the clock, he can first observe a day shift for several days, then evenings and then nights, for a period of consecutive days until he is reasonably familiar with all three shifts. Or he may cover events at any given sub-site by "overlapping" time on consecutive dates—for example, 7:00 A.M. to 9:00 A.M., 8:00 A.M. to 10.00 A.M., 9:00 A.M. to 11:00 A.M.—and over a period of days cover the organization around the clock. These tactical decisions will be made on any of several grounds: the researcher's other (nonresearch) obligations, sleeping habits, tolerance for dealing with different kinds of phenomena, and so on. Such methodical sampling will continue profitably only to the point of general familiarity; but also—or mainly—until the researcher has developed hypotheses or theoretical propositions whose importance demands increasingly, or from time to time, a reordering of his own schedules.

In situations where staffing patterns provide shift breaks and successions of personnel, however, the researcher will be certain to observe and to listen at these critical moments or events; for the personnel on each shift will be busy representing to each other, as realities, what transpired during the preceding time periods (which the researcher may or may not have observed directly that day). Also, timed observations will "tell" the researcher not only of 24-hour activity, but what occurs on weekends as against weekdays, Saturdays as against Sundays. These may be quite as different as the day is from the night. The researcher's increasing understanding of the time dimension in terms of events will affect his own operational decisions bearing upon the temporal dimension.

Deciding on a research location

Now a brief discussion bearing on the sampling of space or place. Of course the researcher must make critical decisions about *where* he should locate himself at any given time. There is a relationship between a location and the kinds of information and events that will come within his line of sight. Therefore, he constantly must ask himself, and others, where he should be; also in any specific location where he should stand or move about—indeed, whether he should follow particular persons who move (whose job it may be to move) from one situation or locale to another. Every decision will affect what kinds of events will come to his attention. The researcher must also consider that informal bits of evidence about the very location he is observing might actually be offered elsewhere, such as in a lounge or dining area.

Inevitably the researcher discovers that while he was observing at one sub-site something happened at another that was more "significant" for his research; he may curse inwardly because he missed being at the event. Again, no matter—he made his decision to be where he was, and now must stick by it. At other times, the researcher begins to wonder whether he should not leave his current observation post, even though he may have been at it only an hour or so, because "nothing seems to be happening" that isn't familiar. He asks himself, "Shouldn't I be expending my energies elsewhere?" It is just such decisions over which novices anguish, but actually they need not. They must learn to live with the reality that is research, as is life—while such decisions must be made, proper selective sampling eventually will meet their most stringent research requirements.

All this suggests decisions among *single, multiple* and *mobile* positioning, and alternations among these. Obviously, a single position yields a relatively narrow perspective, even though the researcher is picking up a variety of cues about what is going on elsewhere, particularly as these events impinge upon the single station. There are some advantages, however, to "staying put" for longer periods: the researcher stabilizes time as well as place (eventful time elsewhere may be quite different); also he gains the advantage of having greater familiarity with those who work at this specific site (they may find it easy to explain their work to someone interested enough to tarry).

Multiple positioning has its advantages, too. It provides comparative data of all sorts, and allows the researcher to raise hypotheses about relations among people at different locations; he gets wider perspective. Also, he can move about, particularly in the early stages, using movement as a tactic for giving "relief" to persons in any given location who communicate their unease at being observed. There is also a tactic of *tracing* wherein the researcher attaches himself to a single person (of a class of people) and follows him or them about through the entire course of a single task, or even an entire work shift. (We say more about this tactic in a later chapter.)

In connection with the sampling of locations, the observer also may have in mind sampling *things,* such as instruments or other equipment located in special rooms. These are pertinent to given tasks at the site, and although ultimately related to people and activity, they may constitute a kind of spatial sample because of their location.

The various tactics of spatial observation are by no means mutually exclusive; they compliment each other and present an almost infinite variety of opportunities—also some headaches and hard decisions concerning where to be at any given time. Again, randomness has little value; interest and emergent opportunities have priority.

Sampling people

In his sampling of people, the researcher works from a sociologically axiomatic base: that in any human organization, people stand in different relationships to the whole of that organization, in some important respects probably viewing and using it differently; and that these differences can be gleaned from what people say and how they act. While the researcher anticipates meeting certain classes of persons at the site or the sub-site, certain existential properties of people will be "presented" to him, and also he understands that probably he will discover classes of people not initially obvious to him. Certainly he could do the sampling task randomly; but again he has selected samples in mind, and probably in such density as to insure the necessary coverage of all the important or at least obvious ones. He will probably select from among the universe of people according to their functions *for his research*. Thus, if his perspective and interests are predominantly historical, his central selective principle may be seniority in the organization: old-timers and new-comers have entered the stream of organizational history at different points. They have had not only different past experiences but now experience the movement or the organization differently by virtue of their respective differences in time of entry—and probably also because of qualitative differences in their organizational commitments. On the other hand if the researcher's interest bears mainly on the exercise of power, probably he will give higher priority —greater sampling chance—to the category of "echelon." Likewise, other categories (such as age, sex, status, role or function in the organization, or even stated philosophy or ideology) might operate as departures for selective sampling. Our researcher is quite aware that his own activity might, and probably will, lead to discoveries of *new* categories. Hence, those regarded earlier of relative unimportance may become extremely important. For example, *sex differentiation* may appear initially of no importance but later the researcher realizes that important differences exist within the organization by virtue of sex; consequently he develops appropriate hypotheses and so plans more thorough sampling by that particular dimension.

Sampling events

Another dimension that the researcher finds very important concerns *events or situations*. In truth, this dimension is at the heart of his research insofar as time, place, and even people represent—sociologically speaking —merely a context for situations and activities. There is a universe of situations or events from which the researcher can sample. Generally speaking, events or situations are of three orders: routine, special, and untoward. To the extent the human organization that he is studying is institutionalized, it will undoubtedly have many routine events, but even social movements will have some of these. Routine events are regularly scheduled situations wherein people meet to work or to discuss their activities. These situations include all regular meetings, conferences, and ordinary daily activities or work. Special events include fortuitous but anticipated occurrences, which, though not necessarily routine, are organized for moving the organization through successive stages of its activities. There are special meetings, outings, prearranged visits by outsiders, and the like. Untoward events include those that are entirely unanticipated, of an emergency nature, or to some extent anticipated but untimed. Clearly the situational dimension is highly interrelated with the temporal and spatial dimensions.

The easiest and most obvious procedure is to obtain lists of scheduled events that occur during any given period, such as a week, and selectively sample each event. Situations are, in fact, of such critical importance that the researcher might not even sample; he might take the entire universe— so that he is assured of having observed at least once every routine event which occurs in the organization. Later, he can establish the importance of any of these events, and decide how many successive visits and observations he would need before he could fully understand the implications of each event. In the course of these visits and participations, the researcher will hear of special events upcoming and will take pains to attend and observe at these, for he can expect that special events have special implications for the participants. To the extent that either is at any given location within the organization or moving about, he is in a position to witness untoward events. And if not actually there in the midst of a unique occurrence, he will have people at hand with whom he can speak about what had actually occurred—usually picking up a variety of perspectives on any given occurrence. He can maximize this variety by seeking out persons whom he anticipates might have differential perspectives, including those that represent people low in hierarchy or tending to hold marginal or "peculiar" views.

The Task and the Resources to Do It

The researcher has just about finished his mapping procedures and now has an opportunity to look more fully at the task he has set for himself. On a closer look probably the task has presented him with new properties: technical problems, and intellectual or research opportunities that he had not anticipated. Any of these possibilities may have altered his original foci of interest—sharpened or shifted them. In fact, this is a critical juncture in his research, for he will find it necessary to measure the task (as a result either of prior expectation or new revelation) that he wishes to accomplish against his available resources. These resources include mundane but very important factors such as his own time, energy, and money—the last mentioned bearing on whether he can hire research or clerical assistants.

The researcher knows he must make some difficult decisions, but he can employ a number of alternate tactical plans. Let us imagine first several new problems in his research. One obvious problem is that "the thing" is bigger than he had originally thought: the institution is more complex than anticipated. Perhaps the social movement has unanticipated dimensions of ideology and organizational activity, or the movement once thought distinctive is now found to be intricately tied to another movement. Also, as the researcher moved about among locales and among advocates of the social movement, he had found it too scattered spatially for the kind of work he imagined he would be doing, or so ephemeral that locations as well as people are very mobile and therefore elusive. Perhaps he would need far more time than anticipated to search for events and people, and perhaps many have no phones nor even stable addresses. In institutional research, an equivalent problem may be the difficulty of making appointments to see people and even to locate them within rooms and corridors. Such problems threaten the researcher's entire timetable. Additional difficulties that may befall any researcher are easily conjured up.

Of course, these problems are variously difficult or significant as defined by a researcher in terms of his own personal properties. He must count his pennies, find an automobile that will give the needed mobility to track down respondents; also he must assess his own talent, skills and motivations for tracking people down, and for persuading them to talk freely and to accept him as a sort of constant companion. Can he indeed change his sleeping habits and alter his schedule of relations with family and friends? Does he have the patience and the thickness of skin necessary to find people and to persuade them to cooperate? In short, this is a time when the researcher must negotiate with himself.

In handling the above problems, the researcher has a number of options. He can narrow his focus and settle on only one rather than two or three important questions that he might ask about his object of inquiry. After all, a little earlier he may have found that some of his initial ideas were not very clever or profound; even have discovered some new and potentially more fruitful foci of interest. Now is the time to seize the opportunity actually to restructure interests and simultaneously tailor the task more realistically to one's resources and talents. Perhaps now he can sacrifice some breadth for depth of coverage, concentrating on a narrower range—though he may not if he finds good reasons not to do so.

Another option is to increase the number and depth of interviews, but reduce somewhat the time devoted to observation. After all, when one measures the cost-effectiveness of interviewing against observation, the former is more economical. The researcher need not, however, abandon observation; he will still do it but mainly to test what he hears, rather than primarily to discover something new that way. Certainly, for social movements in early development there is relatively little to observe. As for institutional life and work where ideology and operational philosophy are fairly well articulated, the researcher can skillfully pit one interview against another and only sparingly observe his respondents in action to insure the validity of their remarks. Also, following his mapping tour and initial assessment of the task, he may have become sufficiently savvy to develop a brief but incisive questionnaire covering a number of points salient to his interests. This would give him at least some of the breadth he wants, but with some economy in time—having covered everyone in small but significant measure he then can concentrate on fewer key people. Of course this option may have to be weighed against his promise not to make any or much work for his host. But didn't the chief want some answers to certain fundamental questions in line with the researcher's initial objectives?

Finally, he may secure assistance in the form of a *research team* if he has the requisite money—he may be able to buy time in order to do the job as he wishes. Or, he may be able to persuade some colleagues to join him, each taking a focus for himself although sharing data with all. A division of labor not only is time saving but can be productive conceptually, insofar as each can make an original contribution or simply function as a sounding board for another's ideas. Under team conditions, contributions tend to mulptiply rather than add up, and multiple researchers have the advantages of a built-in and rapid corrective to false ideas, which would take considerable time or at least more time to correct alone. Also, many blind operational alleys are avoided through mutual counsel. Yet, team work is not all positive. A lone researcher perhaps ought not to be dissuaded from pursuing an intriguing idea, or ought not to have to concern himself with compromises for the sake of "adjustment" to the personalities and hang-ups of colleagues. If the assistants are not "true" colleagues but have quite different conceptual frameworks, then considerable difficulty in cooperation is encountered. Likewise, if the assistants are not genuine equals but hired hands without much theoretical or methodological sophistication, then the chief researcher would need to train, monitor, and supervise them, and thereby do too little actual fieldwork for his own satisfaction.

All the above problems and options further depend on the researcher's degree of familiarity with the general activities and vocabularies of the scene or "world" that he is observing. When he is quite familiar with the scene, his observations and his interviews need not cover every aspect of activity or nuance of verbal meaning. He already has appreciable definition and conceptual grasp of the situation. We say this in the face of our own admonitions to students not to take meanings for granted, but to probe for them. However, the skilled and knowledgeable researcher will probe for nuance selectively, either because he doesn't yet understand something fully enough or is intent upon finding shades of difference among his respondents. To the extent that he knows reasonably well some of the major vocabulary of the persons in the particular world under study, he need not probe for the meanings of every term. But if the activities and vocabularies which structure the scene are new and perhaps strange, then the researcher has no recourse but to plumb their meanings. The option then to reduce the scope of study makes some sense. For those researchers who feel deeply that they must have a reasonably good grasp of the whole in order to research any part of it, the problem of encompassing the whole can be handled through highly selective interviews of a few key people coupled with selective observations. The mapping tour itself may be enough to provide sufficient context for whatever specific aspect or problem is being researched.

Of course, we are writing here in the light of possible "compromises" which may be required—given real limitations in time and other resources —yet a word is necessary bearing on the overall question of time in relation to "depth." In an older tradition of scholarship and thoroughness, particularly as developed in anthropology, the researcher set virtually no (or very long) time limits to his work in an effort to plumb the very depths of the culture under study. This length of time may be necessary for no other reason than that language systems have to be understood reasonably well before other aspects of culture can be understood. We do not need to follow this model in its purest form (nor do all social anthropologists). We can assume that our researcher has had some experiences—perhaps vicariously—with the phenomenon in question, some acquaintanceship with its special vocabulary, and above all probably the sense enough to know that he will not "get it all." (Again, we shall return to this topic in the chapter on analysis.)

Later we shall refer to a concept of "spinning off," wherein a researcher abstracts pieces of the whole over time, assuming that he wishes to go on and on as in a "lifetime" of work. For the most part, and realistically, researchers first will get a general picture and then focus on one or two special problems but only until their satisfactory completion. With some preplanning and especially with inclusion of such procedures as "casing" and "mapping," the researcher will know how much he can reasonably accomplish in any given period of time. We recall our having briefly visited and mapped eight semiautonomous treatment wards at a state hospital, and not having the time to study each to our satisfaction. What to do? Study everyone less thoroughly? Select three or four by strictly random number? But we had indeed visited them all and already knew enough about each to take a meaningful—that is, theoretically fruitful—sample. Since our foci of interests included treatment ideology as well as organization and operations, we developed a simple classificatory scheme which yielded four classes and one unique, nondescript case. One class offered three cases, of which we selected the ideological archetype; another class offered two cases of which we again selected the archetype. These selections, then, allowed us to screen out three questionably productive cases. Finally, we selected the nondescript case because, we felt, the uniqueness of its structure would yield data of theoretical importance to the understanding of the entire lot of wards. This is how we were able to conceptualize the whole and tailor it to the resources available to us.

Where Does One Start and When?

We have already indicated that when researching a social movement the observer begins his research with his first contact, wherever that may be, and makes his way from there by depending upon successive informants to guide or cue him to other persons and places. Initially, at least, there is little problem about when and where to start. If researching a new social movement, the researcher often has relatively few initial cues and leads, therefore works quite pragmatically and often depends primarily upon fortuitous circumstances. Eventually, through his effective interviewing, informants will offer him multiple opportunities for watching and listening. He will recognize that he is being offered options and will select them in sequence according to the requirements of any given stage of his research. Generally, he moves towards observing the ideological and organizational leadership and the larger and more stable clusterings of advocates.

In organizational research, where locations of activity and of groups are reasonably well laid out through the mapping process, care has to be given to where and when to "start." The decision concerning where to start has special importance, for it bears upon the relationships existing among organizational segments and their relative power and prestige—particularly between the formal administrative leadership and other echelons. Since the researcher has come through the front office, probably he will decide to start his research there for at least two good reasons.

First, he must eventually—the sooner the better—separate himself from the leadership by publicly establishing his independence in the research and in all his social relations on the job. Thus, if he is to study central administration at all he might well begin there. Then, either he leaves it and does not return until the end of his work, or visits there only intermittently, depending on his research purposes. In any event, the researcher must *not* appear to be reporting findings and may have to take special pains to prove that he is not. The researcher actually will tell people elsewhere about his independence and his respect for each and all groups; but he must demonstrate his honesty by actions as well as by assertion. It may take a bit of time before he earns trust.

The second reason for starting with the central administration is that it can provide a special overview of the entire operation, including its intended work, the rationale for it and its organization. Here, the researcher can get a history of the organization, and a "view from the top" bearing upon the present state and future plans of the organization—a view possibly neither fully shared with nor agreed upon by any other segment of the organization. Of course, this view, however apparently complete and "straight from the horse's mouth," is no more true or real than any other view; but it is one (or several depending upon the number of persons there) that provides a good working start for the researcher.

Following his observations and conversations with the leadership, the researcher returns to those people and places that he visited while mapping. His observational schedules reflect his current substantive interests, sampling plans, and estimates of personnel receptivity. If he has not already done so he will arrange, as he moves from one site to the next, to start there when most persons are present to hear him tell at least briefly of his work and of his independence. This is not at all difficult to arrange: in most service institutions the personnel meet frequently as teams.

In deciding to begin observing at any given sub-site, the researcher utilizes a number of tactics that takes into account the readiness of people to be observed. He has recognized *differences in receptivity* among the various people at the sub-sites, knowing that members at some sites require more time to get ready for him, or perhaps require time to hear that no untoward or threatening events have occurred as a consequence of his presence elsewhere. Once relatively good relations have been established, he will be a frequent visitor there, for he finds it advantageous to keep the relationship "warm." Indeed, his disappearance from any sub-site for too many days, sometimes even for hours, will cool relationships. Once people accept the researcher they want him to be present at their work—and expect him to be there. Many a researcher, though relatively saturated with data or concerned with planning his next steps, will visit a sub-site regularly not so much to observe as to maintain good relations until he can put a closure to a given set of observations. This tactic may not be necessary at later stages of the research when and if most people generally have accepted him, although if he expects to return again at all to the sub-site he may still have to plead being very busy pursuing his research interests elsewhere. However, his relatively continuous presence or at least occasional revisits will surely yield excellent results; once respondents take the researcher into account as a symbolic reference they will regularly tell him of things missed between his visits: "you should have been here this morning! . . ."

All the above remarks apply to organizational research and also to research into social movements, whose sub-sites are spatially separate but not so distant that they cannot easily be visited. If the researcher is studying a social movement or an organization whose sub-sites are geographically dispersed (as in "branches"), then he may treat each as a kind of separate site which possesses its own sub-sites. There is an exception, however, and that is when the branches are so small as to constitute only a small group of people; seemingly then they have no sub-sites. Their absence may be more apparent than real, since even small groups usually have sub-groupings of persons who can be discovered meeting informally either in spatial areas of "the same place" or outside the organization's work place or the social movement's office or meeting place.

Suggested Reading

There is a paucity of good (or extensive) discussion on "getting started." However, in various monographs one can see the field worker in the early stages of the organization of his work. Listed below are a number of excellent monographs chosen both for their range of substantive focus and for their information (unfortunately sometimes too sparse) on starting and organizing processes.

Sociologists

BECKER, HOWARD, BLANCHE GEER, and E. HUGHES, *Making the Grade.* New York: John Wiley & Sons, 1968.

BECKER, HOWARD, BLANCHE GEER, E. HUGHES, and A. STRAUSS, *Men in White.* Chicago: University of Chicago Press, 1961.

BOTT, ELIZABETH, *Family and Social Network.* London: Tavistock Publishing Co., 1957.

CAVAN, SHERRY, *Liquor License.* Chicago: Aldine Publishing Co., 1966.

CRESSEY, PAUL G., *The Taxi Dance Hall.* Chicago: University of Chicago Press, 1932.

DALTON, MELVILLE, *Men Who Manage.* New York: John Wiley & Sons, 1959.

DOLLARD, JOHN, *Caste and Class in a Southern Town.* New York: Doubleday & Co., 1937.

FOX, RENEE, *Experiment Perilous.* New York: The Free Press, 1959.

GANS, HERBERT, *The Levittowners.* New York: Pantheon Books, 1967.

GLASER, B., and A. STRAUSS, *Awareness of Dying.* Chicago: Aldine Publishing Co., 1965.

HUGHES, EVERETT, *French Canada in Transition.* Chicago: University of Chicago Press, 1963.

HUMPHRIES, LAUD, *Tearoom Trade.* Chicago: Aldine Publishing Co., 1970.

LEWIS, HYLAND, *Blackways of Kent.* Chapel Hill, N.C.: University of North Carolina Press, 1955.

LIEBOW, ELLIOT, *Tally's Corner.* Boston: Little, Brown and Co., 1967.

LOFLAND, JOHN, *Doomsday Cult.* Englewood Cliffs, N.J.: Prentice-Hall, 1966.

LYND, R., and D. LYND, *Middletown.* New York: Harcourt Brace Jovanovich, 1929).

OLESEN, VIRGINIA, and E. WHITTAKER, *The Silent Dialogue.* San Francisco: Jossey-Bass, 1968.

RAINWATER, LEE, et al., *Behind Ghetto Walls.* Chicago: Aldine Publishing Co., 1970.

ROTH, JULIUS, *Timetables.* Indianapolis: Bobbs-Merrill, 1963.

SEELEY, J., R. SIM, and E. LOOSLEY, *Crestwood Heights.* New York: John Wiley & Sons, 1963.

STANTON, ALFRED, and MORRIS SCHWARTS, *The Mental Hospital.* New York: Basic Books, 1954.

STRAUSS, A., L. SCHATZMAN, R. BUCHER, D. ERLICH, and M. SABSHIN, *Psychiatric Ideologies and Institutions.* New York: The Free Press, 1964.

SUDNOW, DAVID, *Passing On.* Englewood Cliffs, N.J.: Prentice-Hall, 1967.

SUTTLES, GERALD, *The Social Order of the Slum.* Chicago: University of Chicago Press, 1968.

VIDICH, A., and J. BENSMAN, *Small Town in Mass Society.* New York: Doubleday & Co., 1960.

VOGEL, EZRA, *Japan's New Middle Class.* Berkeley: University of California Press, 1967.

WHYTE, WILLIAM F., *Street Corner Society.* Chicago: University of Chicago Press, 1941. Revised edition, 1955.

YOUNG, MICHAEL, and PETER WILLMOTT, *Family and Kinship in East London.* Baltimore: Penguin Books, 1962.

Anthropologists

ARENSBERG, CONRAD, *The Irish Countryman.* New York: The Macmillan Company, 1942.

BEALS, ALAN, *Gopalur: A South Indian Village.* New York: Holt, Rinehart and Winston, 1970.

BERRAMAN, GERALD, *Behind Many Masks: Ethnography and Impression Management in a Himalayan Village.* Ithaca, N.Y.: Sociological Applied Anthropology, Monograph #4, 1962.

practically and technically, no observation or experience becomes a datum until it can be put to use as background or context, as a discovered property or feature of a scene, or as a detail which helps clarify or define a class of events. At first, because the researcher will not know how he will eventually code or sort out his many observations, he will probably record considerably more than he will ever use directly. He knows, more intuitively than by design, that many events observed early will "achieve" meaning at a later time. For this reason, and because at this stage he wants to do more "sponging up" (of sights and sounds) than "spewing out" (of interpretations), his observations are governed appreciably by events that naturally present themselves. He attends to people: their numbers, dress, general deportment, and humor. He attends to physical setting: equipment, space, wall posters, and even noise levels. He attends to events or activities: work, play, the vigor of engagement, arguments and discussions, how many work alone or in teams. All these and more are noted, with many of their qualitative and quantitative attributes.

Novices in research worry too soon about developing salient categories for final analysis, about developing brilliant concepts, and about establishing "patterns of interaction"; in short, they want quickly to prove to themselves and others that they are social scientists. Not so our model researcher; he is quite content, for a considerable time, to experience the ambience of the scene. He has great patience, as well as a tolerance for ambiguity and for his own immediate ignorance. Far from acting like a scientist and telling himself he is one, he is genuinely busy being a learner—indeed, a novice— and perhaps a participant.

For a time, at least, the researcher may ignore his sampling schedules and concern himself simply with decisions on whether to stand, sit, or move about for a better look-see, or to eavesdrop. Also, he is taking the measure of emerging properties which will affect his subsequent operations: Are the people shy or afraid? How closely can he station himself to an activity? How actively or penetratingly, at this time, can he raise questions about what he sees? Thus, the selectivity of his perceptions is grounded in different perspectives and methodological needs, and from time to time he shifts these grounds with considerable control. Where at first he may attend to the density of the population and the pace of its activity, as well as identify what it is doing, he may later shift concern to his sampling schedule. But in truth, we are at a loss here in describing how any researcher may sequence his observation. For fear that readers may try to seize upon *our* reference to sequencing and thus deduce a pattern—and probably spoil their own native senses of timing and sequencing—we shall simply list some of the many grounds for observation, not attempting to establish a logical sequence for their use.

DAVIS, ALLIS, et al., *Deep South*. Chicago: University of Chicago Press, 1941.

DuBois, CORA, *The People of Alor*. Minneapolis: University of Minnesota Press, 1944.

EVANS-PRITCHARD, E., *Witchcraft, Oracles and Magic Among the Azande*. New York: Oxford University Press, 1937.

————, *The Nuer*. Oxford: Clarendon Press, 1940.

FIRTH, RAYMOND, *We, The Tikopia*. London: Allen and Unwin, 1936.

FORTES, MEYER, *The Web of Kinship Among the Tallensi*. London, New York: Published for the International African Institute by the Oxford University Press, 1949.

GALLAGHER, ARTHUR, *Plainville Fifteen Years After*. New York: Columbia University Press, 1961.

GEERTZ, CLIFFORD, *Peddlers and Princes*. Chicago: University of Chicago Press, 1963.

HITCHCOCK, JOHN, *The Magars of Banyan Hill*. New York: Holt, Rinehart and Winston, 1966.

JOSEPH, ALICE, ROSAMOND SPICER, and JANE CHESKY, *The Desert People: A Study of the Papago Indians*. Chicago: University of Chicago Press, 1949.

KLUCKHOHN, CLYDE, and DOROTHEA LEIGHTON, *The Navaho*. Cambridge, Mass.: Harvard University Press, 1961.

LEACH, EDMUND, *Political Systems of Highland Burma: A Study of Kachin Social Structure*. Cambridge, Mass.: Harvard University Press, 1954.

————, *Pul Eliya: A Village in Ceylon*. Cambridge, England: Cambridge University Press, 1961.

LEWIS, OSCAR, *Life in a Mexican Village*. Urbana, Ill.: University of Illinois Press, 1951.

MALINOWSKI, B., *Argonauts of the Western Pacific*. New York: E. P. Dutton, 1961.

PHILLIPS, H., *Thai Peasant Personality*. Berkeley: University of California Press, 1965.

REDFIELD, ROBERT, *The Folk Culture of Yucatán*. Chicago: University of Chicago Press, 1941.

SPIRO, MELFORD E., *Kibbutz: Venture in Utopia*. Cambridge, Mass.: Harvard University Press, 1956.

WARNER, W. LLOYD, *A Black Civilization*. New York: Harper & Row, 1937. Revised edition, 1958.

————, *The Social Life of a Modern Community*. New Haven, Conn.: Yale University Press, 1941.

4

Strategy for Watching

First Impressions

Our discussions of watching will be rather arbitrarily and artificially separated from listening, because each has some unique aspects bearing upon the gathering of data. Yet, we know that watching and listening are closely linked; the researcher is using all his senses simultaneously and also thinking (analyzing). In the field, the "input" of experience is exceedingly high, and however selectively it may be received through a sensory system, there is an internal interchange and a reflective transformation of these experiences. Awareness of this experiential input is particularly apparent to the researcher in the first hours of observation; hence he will take advantage of his initial sensitivities because he knows that within a short time they may be significantly lost to familiarity and to adjustment quite as they have long since been lost to persons indigenous to the places that he visits. First observations—indeed, merely "sensings," of sights, sounds, smells, touch and even of taste—form a special class of experience. Although at first these experiences may be little more than impressions—a product derived as much from the observer as from the observed—they often have considerable value for later description and analysis.

The researcher's awareness of and capitalization on his sensitivity is per-

haps his most valued resource and tool for discovery. Let us look at four related components of sensitivity. First, people who work at anything for relatively long periods lose sensitivity to common, recurrent experiences and tend to thrust them into the background, if for no other reason than that they get in the way of whatever else they are immediately sensitive to. This is why any outsider (researcher or other) has some advantage in the observation and analysis of events and structures; he can see properties "lost" to insiders, relate them to still other properties, and thereby discover something of value to theory or to his hosts.

Second, far from depending upon only the first moments of "culture shock" for his descriptive and analytic stimulation, *the researcher strives to maintain a continuing "de novo" sensitivity and appreciation of all events*. Ironically, his very effort to become selective runs counter to this principle. Yet, generally a loss in sensitivity, such as boredom, represents a failure of active relations between the observer and the observed; hence the researcher seeks to make capital of even the most ordinary and repetitive events, either to wrest something new from them or to use them to test an idea. It helps also to be visiting or staying at more than one sub-site simultaneously, for this sharpens contrast and tends to make the researcher wonder more about the seemingly familiar.

Third, *the researcher is particularly sensitive to his own interpreted experience*. Even the most subtle of his own surprises—whether of delight or disappointment, but especially of incomprehensibility—is a sign that some expectation or hypothesis of his has been altered or even shattered. He asks himself "why," and pursues the import of his own response through active inquiry. This also is how the researcher maintains his necessary state of wonder and excitement even though his substantive materials may seem most mundane.

Fourth, *the researcher also does his best to capitalize on whatever sensitivities may be yielded by his past experiences,* of whatever kind. While these experiences (transposed too liberally or literally to the current scene) may lead him astray, initially they can be a rich source of sensitivities whose validity can later be checked upon. At first those sensitivities only have the status of hypotheses, but possibly fruitful ones. To entirely repress past experiences and their associated observational consequences is neither possible nor useful for the researcher.

Grounds for Watching

Presenting properties

These last comments especially lead to a new problem: to what will the researcher attend, and how does he decide which of his new and varied observations and experiences might or should constitute his data? Both

In addition to the most existential grounds (presenting properties) for observational selection, others command attention: representativeness, perspective, framework, listening, theoretical leads, and verification.

Representativeness is embodied in the plans for sampling which the researcher has already made. This ground provides not only a general basis for observational selection but a defense against input-flooding, whimsical observation, or fruitless and unwitting bias. Since we have already briefly discussed the researcher's concern with representativeness and coverage, we can proceed to the other grounds for observation.

Perspective is a relatively difficult concept to deal with; many researchers often fail to make a clear distinction between it and theoretical framework. Taken by itself—that is, without the often used prefix "theoretical"—it opens to us an almost limitless land of "angles," for perspective refers to an *angle of observation*. Like it or not, man is condemned to viewing from one (or more) perspectives or angles, as reality is infinitely complex and no observer can see it all. In "truth," all observation then takes on a biased hue. For the field researcher, the matter of bias is accepted; his concern is directed at the fruitfulness of observation from any given angle. Given intelligence and skill adequate to the task, he will frequently shift from one angle of observation to another, and assess their relative value to his work. Thus, his observations, though biased, are certainly witting (understood and controlled), and often fruitful of results for his research.

The difficulty in defining perspective is compounded by the fact that several perspectives can be used simultaneously: the perspective of a stated sub-unit or any single actor, of the leadership or the entire organization, and so on. Then, there are perspectives inherent in the observer that probably relate closely to his personal view of man and human life as tragic, humorous, ridiculous, pathetic, and the like. These too will undoubtedly influence not only what he will attend to, but how he will conceptualize. Also, the researcher can look at his activities artistically, scientifically, or "philosophically," and these break down into sub-perspectives. Within the scientific perspective further shifts can be made; he can observe as an economist, political scientist, or anthropologist. What he sees from each of these will significantly vary from the others. Sometimes it helps—especially if events seem too ordinary or situations grow too rapidly familiar —deliberately to adopt one or another of such perspectives as noted above.

Framework. When one adds the concept "theoretical" to that of perspective, he has added another element of control that is rooted in a general theory or network of mutually supporting theories. A set of interrelated concepts is thereby provided that constitutes an additional perspective and provides a framework for conceptual entrée. A relatively encompassing structure of concepts helps organize experience and provides many research questions. From our own theoretical framework, we cannot imagine any noteworthy observations occurring without a minimal set of social science categories: social structure, ideology, work, social control, and so on. Such concepts do not necessarily predispose the observer to the direct use or test of any given theory; rather, they provide only some initial order for observing activities that might otherwise seem chaotic. Hopefully, these categories will, in time, move into the background as they are supplemented, or preferably supplanted, by grounded concepts more descriptive and analytic of the activities actually observed.

Just a few comments are necessary to show the relation between *listening* and *watching*. Even the most astute watching, by itself, will yield limited and often questionable results, particularly because of the complexity and unfamiliarity of the new site, and the limited time available for watching. No observer can escape the necessity of applying categories which identify and give meaning to whatever he is observing. Without verbal indicators from others, he must supply them for himself. Even were he well read on the subject under study, unless his categories were grounded in situations practically identical to those under observation, he is likely to be in trouble. Of course, he might be satisfied with a very superficial order of description; but even then he would probably not enjoy an adequate test of his description. He would tend to project his own "feelings" about the situation into his description and to impute inadequate or even incorrect motives to the people whom he has observed.

Also, watching by itself is quite uneconomical in the expenditure of time when compared to listening; probably this is why there are so many field interview studies of human situations and few, if any, done by watching alone. Yet, once verbal indicators are given to the observer, particularly by persons who normally act in the given situation, the gain from watching after even a few remarks is considerable. For example, the native actor provides a corrective to designation and meaning: "But the nurse is not just playing cards with the patient, she is making contact, establishing trust, and forming a meaningful relationship with the patient." Another example, this one bearing upon an observation missed: "But we do take into account the patient's physical health; each is given an examination at the time of admission." Such verbal comments provide names for things, indicate relationships between them, reveal sequences and presumed causal or logical connections, and provide meaningful context. They tell the observer where and when to look, what precisely to look for; and generally make his observations more astute. Sophistication enables the observer to ask more intelligent and incisive questions, and his observation gains accordingly.

Theoretical leads

When the researcher enters the field, he harbors, wittingly or not, many expectations, conjectures, and hypotheses which provide him with thought and directives on what to look for and to ask about. He has had a good start if he is at all aware of some of these hypotheses. But soon, many of these are disposed of, either because they prove false or lose significance. Simultaneously the researcher is developing new hypotheses, as he identifies the properties of the scene and attempts to relate them variously to each other; he begins, thereby, to develop propositions about what he sees and hears. These propositions, however tentative, constitute sets of hypotheses which function as leads to still other observations—not necessarily "new" ones, but possibly repeats from another perspective—since he is now asking different sorts of questions. Likewise, he is now looking for, or at, things that he had missed just previously, for without the new lead he simply did not see something that is now important to him. Some of these theoretical leads may take on such importance as to suggest major revisions in research objectives, including sampling plans and original problems or foci of attention. However the researcher may deal with these leads, as commands or enticements, he has to take them into account and reorder at least some of his watching operations. This is what observation in the context of discovery is all about.

The need for *verification* and its effect upon watching operations ought to be quite obvious. In the back of his mind, if not in the forefront, the researcher is concerned with the validity of his observations. His entire research enterprise, however pleasurable, is not a "lark"; it is organized and systematized work eventually leading to publication. In the context of his collegial relations, wider audiences, the requirements of science, and the "report" he owes his host about their own work, the researcher attends to the validation of at least the more significant propositions that will constitute his analysis. In a most general sense, every afterthought and second glance is an act of verification and certainly this is even more true for the attention paid to his key propositions. These are so critical, in fact, that towards the end of the study, most of the researcher's time is devoted towards a search for additional (including negative) evidence bearing upon them. His watching then is intensely focused ("pinpointed") and organized considerably differently from the way it was at early phases of the research. (For instance, in the study of psychiatric ideologies, the fieldworkers developed the notion of "negotiated order" in the hospital— a place where many people were negotiating with each other in order to get jobs done. The fieldworkers, having developed those ideas, began a series of pinpointing operations. Staff were questioned about their special arrangements or understandings with one another. This kind of interviewing involved special focus, not only on negotiation but on how already known and studied staff relationships impinged on negotiations—and vice versa. Similarly, in the same study, the fieldworkers observed patient interactions in very special, focused ways near the end of the study; although their aim was to study staff ideologies, they recognized rather late that information about patients could lend additional weight to their major propositions about staff ideology and its influence on staff behavior. And relatively near the end of the study of terminal care, a suicide occurred on one of the hospital wards. The researchers rushed to that ward—where they had never done any observing—and spent the next few days pinpointing the chronology of events that occurred before, during, and after the suicide. This unfortunate event allowed them to check out what happens when a dying trajectory gets totally "out of whack."

Watching as Active Presence

The presence of a stranger, particularly an observer, in a natural human situation introduces some measure of disturbance in the scene. The researcher is aware of this; he certainly does not want to distort the very processes he wishes to capture conceptually. Much of his deportment, at least initially, is therefore designed to prevent changes that result from his presence. Perhaps he cannot succeed entirely; but he is not overly concerned. He will not be immobilized, nor will he quit unless observation is impossible. Any method that might be used to study situations like these poses special problems; if field research creates disturbance, other methods tend to create artificiality. Our researcher will persist, for he can reasonably expect that in time his presence—eventually seen as no threat —will become integrated and normalized. Then, the life and the work of the people there will go on much as it did before he came. After all, their work and other pursuits are more important to them than merely impressing the researcher. (For instance, the researchers in a study of terminal care in hospitals encountered no problems whatever, although they observed on over thirty wards, in either gaining entrée or being allowed to observe the multitude of actions on those wards. The staffs were just too concerned about the problems of terminal care and too busy caring for the dying to feel self-conscious about being observed.) Anyway, a disturbance occasioned by the presence of the observer need not be seen in a negative light; the "disturbance" may (and often does) prove catalytic by way of revealing aspects of organizational life not easily discovered other-wise. No disturbance—not even an error of deportment—is catastrophic or useless unless it is so bad that the researcher is forced to abandon his research at the site. What this suggests is that the researcher's presence, and the variety of activity options available to him, can be immensely strategic when intelligently controlled, paced, and processed.

As we have said, initially the researcher is both establishing an accept-ing environment and attempting to normalize the situation for his hosts. Once these tasks are accomplished, he can attend to a number of options in terms of their relative usefulness for yielding data. Again, we cannot sequence the options—the novice at research will have to play them by ear; therefore, we shall simply list some options according to a logical progression of the researcher's involvement in the observed situation.

Watching from outside

First, the field researcher remains physically outside the situation; for example as in laboratory situations the researcher may observe participants from behind a one-way mirror. But observing without being observed is virtually impossible to manage in natural social settings. The need to sit in on relatively private discussions, and to ask questions, precludes this tactic as a reasonable option.

Passive presence

Second, the field researcher is present in the situation but decides to observe passively. He does not enter into interaction with participants and avoids as much as possible obtruding himself into the event. For example, he may sit in the corner of a room and not enter into conversation. The flow of events is not appreciably influenced by his activity (although his sheer physical presence may do so). This is an acceptable option, par-ticularly in the early stages of research, also for short spans of time when witnessing events which particularly preoccupy the hosts, or indicate special symbolic importance to them. (Thus, years later, in re-reading his field-notes, one of the authors of *Boys in White* noted how very much in the shadows, how little aggressive, how much the observer rather than the participant he was during the first days in the field.) But this option poses some dangers: the spectre of a relatively impassive observer whether or not taking notes, barely showing appropriate affect or active curiosity, and offering few if any cues as to what he is "really up to," can be very disturbing to the hosts. This option cannot be carried on indefinitely and universally for all situations. For their own comfort, even in the first periods of observation, the hosts will attempt to involve the observer; to induce him to reveal his true interests and particularly, his person. They want to be observed by a partly known person, not by a stranger.

Limited interaction

Third, the researcher engages in minimal, clarifying interaction. In this type of situation, the observer does not set himself apart from the participants. His interventions in the flow of interaction are confined mainly to seeking clarification and the meaning of ongoing events. He does not attempt to direct interaction into channels of his own choosing. This type of activity has two distinct advantages: it gets at meaning, and it meets the expectations of the hosts insofar as the researcher is not only an observer, but is revealed as personable and interested; through his comments or questions his apparent agenda is indicated. The agenda is understandable and appears appropriate; therefore, the observer can be thought of as at least "kind of" a member of the group. This allows them quickly to minimize, even temporarily forget his presence, and thus return the situation nearly to "normal." The option is especially useful when the researcher is wary of intruding his person too obviously, when people are just too busy, or where there is danger to someone in his intruding. (For instance, observations made during surgical operations—in a study of medical students, interns and residents—necessarily had to be made, especially at first, with careful attention to placing oneself where one could not possibly get in the way of the staff. Only later, with more experience in this busy and sometimes tense setting, and with much more trust on the part of the staff, was the researcher invited to "step right up and watch," even ask questions, by the chief surgeon.)

Active control

Fourth, the researcher actively controls interaction along lines designed to provide particular information bearing upon the research. The archetype of this option is the formal interview. As applied to an ongoing situation, the researcher engages in active conversation, not only posing general questions but provocative or challenging ones. There are many meetings and other forms of encounter which can, for a time, or in part, be "usurped" to meet the researcher's need for understanding, beyond what may be revealed on the level of cliché and platitude. The researcher is judiciously directive, albeit warm and positive. If well controlled, this level of participant observation is very stimulating for researcher and hosts alike; for without fear or threat present, an intellectual colleagueship is in formation.

Observer as participant

Fifth, the researcher is a full participant in ongoing activities while simultaneously his identity as a researcher is fully known. This option is far less used than the preceding three, but is feasible under at least two conditions. *First,* the researcher wishes to capitalize on a combination of two kinds of expertise: sociological and nonsociological. An instance might be that of a nurse, trained also as a sociologist, who works on a hospital ward as a nurse while also openly gathering data about features of ward life and interaction. *Second,* the researcher wants to convert a purely sociable role into a combined research and sociable one. An instance might be that of a sociologist who frequents a neighborhood bar, there discovers an incipient social movement, and decides to study that phenomenon, openly telling others of his intentions.

Full participation *as researcher* has several disadvantages which flow from the demanding qualities of the participation itself. The researcher cannot just freely float in space and time but is tied to his work (or other activity) as participant. He cannot pretend to be a learner in early stages of the research, for he is presumed knowledgeable, unless he is doing a kind of work new to him. If his participatory activities are especially demanding of energy or time, or both, then the research work will suffer. The foci and even the range of his attention are also affected, for he is not so easily able to scan the field and decide where to place his attention; that decision may be directed largely by the participatory work in which he is engaged. Regrettably also from the standpoint of his research interests, he may waste considerable time, for not all his participatory work will yield valuable research data. Finally, he is more easily able "to go native," adopting one or another position prevalent among his associates; because he may not be able to balance what he sees, experiences and "feels" by hearing the whole range of views of others involved in the organization or social movement; because his experiences are so overwhelming that he gets "overinvolved" and so falls victim to that intense engagement; and because, being trained or experienced in his participatory activity has so unwittingly absorbed certain viewpoints that his participatory activities tend to reinforce those taken for granted to such an extent that he never thinks to challenge them, to regard them as having the status only of hypotheses.

On the other hand, full participation has some special advantages for the researcher. Not the least is that the researcher may get paid for his participatory work—a consideration when there is no other money forthcoming from his research. (This is why the full-participation option sometimes appeals especially to graduate students.) More important in relation to the research itself is that full participation may allow accessibility to certain situations and information—some not always equally accessible, or not so quickly, to an "outside" researcher. By virtue of participatory activity, the "inside" researcher is right there where things happen, and where members talk about what has happened. Others will talk, argue, confide in him because he is a co-worker, a friend, an actual or potential ally.

Under certain circumstances, like intraorganizational feuding, the development of secret coalitions and decisions—and providing the research can maintain apparent neutrality and confidences—participant colleagues will "spill" their actions and intentions to him, not merely because he is a group member, but because his position as an educated researcher will assure understanding for actions that require it. Finally, there is a potential advantage in running the risk of going native: that is, by actually participating, the researcher gains initial and potentially valuable insights into how it may feel to do the work, and shares with other participants in the collective failures and triumphs of group endeavors.

Participation with hidden identity

Sixth, and finally, the researcher is a full participant in ongoing activities while simultaneously he keeps from the observed his identity as researcher. He acts so as to appear identified with the life and work at the site, and offers no cues that might identify a research role. He accepts work assignments and performs them as does his host. This research tactic our own model researcher will not attempt—and not only for ethical reasons —for with his identity hidden, he has given up much of his mobility, and also loses his option to question his hosts in ways natural to an interviewer. The mobility factor is quite as important as the interviewing loss though perhaps less obvious, since participation coupled with hidden identity constrains an observer to identify principally with certain sub-groups or echelons and prevents easy access, even to observe, across jurisdictional or other lines. How can he "be" a client or patient and observe and question his benefactors? How can he "be" a worker and closely question his leaders?

The researcher does not select from among these options so much as use them (and probably other, even finer, gradations) as a guide. Possibly, in time he will have adopted all except the first and the last options, and combined them as well. These options represent sets of tactical choices, each set functioning somewhat differently according to situational limitations and opportunities. The "situation" here includes not only the ongoing events observed, but the observer's identity while observing, his talents, his research requirements, and even his mood. Tactical selection is governed by answers to such important questions as: Am I getting the data I want and need? Am I and are my hosts comfortable, and acting naturally? Am I able to maintain my identity and conceptual distance? These important considerations tell the researcher which of his many options are most suitable. He is doing quite all right when he can answer these questions affirmatively.

Armed with answers to them he can create options and tactics not even noted here. For example, though our researcher would rather not work for the organization, there is no stricture which prevents him from consulting with some one of his hosts who is himself doing research, or from stuffing envelopes with publicity material; and certainly there is no rule which prevents him from participating quite fully in informal gatherings, parties, and selected ceremonies. Indeed, doing occasional helping work (routine to the member but not necessarily to the researcher) may yield conceptual as well as interpersonal dividends. An instance, helping a nurse in a routine task after a patient has been seen by physician and staff allows her to comment to the researcher on their collective performance, a comment which stimulates him to develop an important concept. (At a psychiatric hospital, the researcher followed the night nursing supervisor wherever she went, or was called, for several hours. The supervisors commented frequently to the researcher about persons and events. As a result, the researcher learned that this functionary not only was vitally important to preventing potential crises at night in the hospital but that this job was spread around during the day among very many staff personnel. This led the researcher to draw a distinction between "emergency control" of difficult patients and the much more difficult problem of "crisis control.")

The Observer Is Observed

Insofar as the researcher is present and active, he himself is subject to observation, and this observation can be expected to affect his work. We have more in mind than deportment in its narrow sense. Deportment can be correct, but yet quite inappropriate: as noted earlier the researcher can sit quietly throughout an entire meeting while the group performs its tasks, yet be so impassive—that is, without vocal or facial expression—as to be disconcerting to the group. Moreover, such behavior would fail to generate data, as well as significantly alter a natural scene. Good deportment alone is not enough. Indeed, for action to be appropriate it must also be functional to the research effort. This last point calls for elaboration, at the risk of breaking the main line of discussion.

The researcher as an observed person provides a seeming paradox. His presence changes the scene, but any failure by him to act appropriately also changes the scene. The question is, What is the real scene which is threatened with change? Who can tell? Granted, in a common-sense way, the observer does not *want* to disturb whatever he would want to see occur naturally, yet "occurrence" is a central property of process, and all the "variables" in a situation are *occurrences in process,* not "things" that would otherwise be there unless disturbed. The field researcher knows experientially that the scenes he is observing are not in all features exactly like others he has observed. More important, he knows that over time they naturally change. He can assume they would have changed without his presence. The paradoxical issue of change and not changed represents a philosophical problem that, perhaps, cannot be genuinely solved, and certainly should preoccupy neither us nor our model fieldworker.

The latter, then, has no other recourse than to act as a field researcher might be expected to act, at least insofar as he has already opted to reveal his combined identity as an observer and outsider. Taking care not to overact (and we must leave a definition of this to the reader), the researcher asks questions, raises issues, even provides humor occasionally, and takes notes openly on proper occasions. In short, he not only acts the observer, but acts humanly. Within this context, he takes the roles of the others towards himself and from this, as well as from his understanding of his research requirements, organizes his actions. It follows that the researcher's actions, while socially appropriate, also are operationally catalytic and tactical. The hosts know that the researcher is present, and after a brief time during which the researcher has set a good stage for observation, they act naturally. The data that are obtained through the observer's judicious but active intervention might not actually be readily available to perception and conception were he *not* actively there. For example, the careers or the ideologies of the hosts are not demonstrably there without his being there; they are created or revealed in and through the interaction of the hosts with the observer.

The researcher is both a participant and observer. As a participant, he is, like anyone else, a group member of a sort. But so is every host a member of a sort; they surely are not all alike, but rather make variable contributions. All the group members express mutual appreciation and understanding, provide each other an audience for expression, develop and selectively share inside jokes, glance knowingly at certain persons and not at others and so on. The principal difference between the researcher as member and all others resides in his activity *as observer*—that is, in his work. The others observe too, but there the similarity ends; his observations are linked to a conceptual framework and to a set of operations that are substantially different from the thought processes and operations of the hosts as observer. His conceptual framework and associated operations function for a very different order of work, and they are shared if at all at his discretion and for his own ends. His distance from the observed is conceptional and operational, not social. Thus as a participant he shares much of the social life and relations, including those which surround and invest any work being done at the site. But his own work is shared only at the very end, when either for ethical reasons or because of an agreement, he shares some of the fruits of his labor, or in some small sense it is shared intermittently during the research in the form of occasional public comments or reports in which he reveals a little of what he sees, knows and thinks about the observed site. Some researchers also agree to "feedback" those findings periodically because of a research design predicated either on studying the consequences of feedback or upon a greater commitment to change the organization than to study it.

A final note on this point, somewhat repetitive but probably useful to the novice: we cannot say precisely what the researcher should or should not do; yet we can say something general about the impression he creates about himself. The researcher is a learner, has patience, is tolerant and sympathetic. He wonders first and judges last; he *appears* to be that way, and *is* that way. Furthermore, he generally accepts whatever he sees and hears at face value; he denigrates no motives. He does not visibly take sides on arguments among members no matter how much he may be invited to do so. He is open to the discovery of whatever is not so obvious to others. He is most considerate, polite, but not shy; he is, in fact, rather tough in the sense that he cannot be put off for too long, nor shamed or coerced. He cannot be bought off or drawn into private arrangements, even to gain the data he needs. He assumes that the hosts ultimately would have it no other way.

Suggested Reading

There is no literature dealing explicitly and systematically with grounds for observation, at least in a manner pertinent to our presentation. However, much has been written on roles which field researchers may take to implement their observations. A small but good list would include the following sources.

GLASER, BARNEY, and ANSELM STRAUSS, "Appendix on Method," pp. 261–65 in *Time for Dying*. Chicago: Aldine Publishing Co., 1968.

Briefly and thoughtfully indicates how existential properties of given scenes (in this case, dying in the hospital) helped shape or dictate observational strategies, which, in turn, facilitated observation.

GOLD, RAYMOND L., "Roles in Sociological Field Observations," *Social Forces* (1958), 217–33. Also in McCall-Simmons, *Issues in Participant Observations: A Text and Reader*. Reading, Mass.: Addison-Wesley Publishing Co., 1969.

A good discussion of the advantages and disadvantages of adopting varying roles for observing and for estabilshing researcher–subject relationships.

JUNKER, BUFORD H., *Field Work: An Introduction to the Social Sciences,* Chapter 3, pp. 32–69. Chicago: The University of Chicago Press, 1960.

An excellent, original source discussion of the many roles (and transitions among them) the field researcher may take, and their relationship to the kinds of information he may obtain.

OLESEN, VIRGINIA L., and ELVI W. WHITTAKER, "Role-Making in Participant Observation: Processes in the Researcher-Actor Relationship," in *Human Organization,* XXVI (1967), 273–81.

An empirically grounded discussion of how reciprocal roles are shaped over time by the interaction between researcher and hosts.

ROY, DONALD, "The Study of Southern Labor Union Organizing Campaigns," in Robert W. Habenstein (ed.), *Pathways to Data: Field Methods for Studying Ongoing Social Organizations,* Chapter XII, pp. 216–44. Chicago: Aldine Publishing Co., 1970.

A partisan but convincing argument for the "participant-as-observer" roles as an effective field technique. In other respects, too, an excellent discussion of personal experiences in the field and their relation to the structure of knowledge.

5

Strategy for Listening

In the preceding chapter we very briefly presented a hypothetical construct: observing without listening. Given our framework, this process really is quite impossible; for if nothing else, the observer is listening to himself tell what he is seeing. He names the things, people and events, and relates them to each other in ways that tell, perhaps, more about how he thinks than about what is "there" to be seen. But this is how he makes "sense" of what is there; how he converts motion into activity.

Then, what if the persons whose motions he interprets name them differently? If the observer is trying to make social science as well as sense for himself, he may be in deep trouble; for as we have said earlier, the researcher's sense (or analysis) must take into account the ways that the actors themselves understand what they are doing. Of course, there are social data and analytic forms that do not necessarily require knowing the perspectives of the actors, for example, certain demographic identities and the comings and goings of people, rates, proportions, and the like. But this is not what our researcher is researching: he requires the meaning of human activities, not merely the motion of objects which only indirectly has social significance. Therefore, the observer listens to (or reads) the symbolic sounds of those whose motions must be understood. He will create his social science "on top of" what he hears and sees.

Listening Without Watching

Perhaps now we can reverse the procedure of the preceding chapter and think about listening *without* watching. Indeed, this latter is more feasible and useful, though there are some drawbacks as we have already indicated: the listener must presume that what he hears is itself empirically grounded; or that the verbalization is not so abstract or idealized, that it obscures the range of activities and nuance that it is supposed to represent. If the researcher lacks background or contextual knowledge about what is being told him, then he can "count" or "discount" only in terms of the logic or plausibility of what is said, or wait until others have been interviewed to check out the informant's statements. If the researcher knows the general scene quite well, through prior experience gained elsewhere, then he has some additional advantage, since he can check what he hears against that experience.

But more than a corrective factor is involved when we say there is a distinct advantage to watching and listening simultaneously. Either watching or listening is capable of generating ideas; when combined, however, one "feeds" upon the other and multiplies ideas not only about what is "there" (as substance) but also about additional or better operations for exploring them (as method)—for example, the *kinds* and *quality* of probes that may be used in interview situations. Moreover the respondent is generally more constrained to detail and explain his understandings and his identity as they relate to the interviewer's queries because he is aware that the listener is also a field observer. This same effect is compounded when the respondent is aware that others in the organization also are being interviewed and observed. Then, the credibility of his remarks and his identity are pitted against both the researcher's observations and those special understandings of his own colleagues which bear upon him.

The researcher will find, initially, that some persons will avoid him, but in time he can expect that they will begin to feel uncomfortable for not having talked to him. Most will have to talk, if only to insure that the observer has gotten "it" (and them) "right." Given the normal situation of hierarchical differentiation, ideological, operational, and even personal differences, the average respondent can be articulate and even eloquent. Of course, the researcher knows that eloquence has no necessary relation to validity; it probably relates better to differentiation and to rhetoric. But that is what he wants: "reality" from the perspective of the actor as respondent; he searches and controls for authenticity of perspective.

The researcher believes "everything" and "nothing" simultaneously. He may nod "yes" at every statement, but the nod is a sign of understanding, not necessarily of agreement. Respondents do not always recognize the difference, it is true; but at least they will respect an attentive if not assenting listener—and, of course, may "spill over more" in attempting to convince him. Indeed, at times (depending on the relationships between respondent and interviewer) the latter will feel free to disagree or dispute: he may even decide to pretend disagreement or at least skepticism in order to elicit additional or more candid statements.

Whatever else may be meant by verbal data, for the researcher their meaning amounts to learning how the persons who are linked to the site reveal their operational and modal realities. Listening has no other function, unless the researcher is content merely to make friends or to join in the work and the sociability. Specifically, what the listener is after are the expressed "is's" and "because's" of his subjects. The "is" reveals their designations of the things, people and events—the objectified content of these people's reality. The "because" reveals the presumed relations among all the designations, the why's and wherefore's, the causes, processes, and reasons—in short, the very logic of their thinking about the content of their reality.

Listening also requires getting behind all of the "you know's" and "et cetera's," and especially, the "of course's" which, though they may facilitate the flow of conversation, nevertheless hide multitudes of "is's" and "because's." Also, when any speakers punctuate their remarks—as we all do from time to time—with a "really," then the researcher is well on his way towards laying out the discriminative array which constitutes the variable realities of the actors. The researcher assumes that some aspects of these numerous realities will reflect the speakers' uniqueness or idiosyncrasies, some aspects will be universally shared. Since the researcher will eventually need to make his own discriminations—his own "is's" and "because's"—he must first attend to those of his hosts.

To grasp the shared and variable properties of this symbolic universe, the researcher must be a good *role-taker;* that is, he must "stand" with each respondent in the latter's relationship to the universe, and view it and its associated vocabulary from that perspective. The role-taking process is the first stage of understanding, requiring systematic listening without applying one's own analytic categories. In a second stage, the listener performs a simple comparative analysis of what he is hearing now, against what others (in this universe) in like or different positions have been telling him. Only then does he engage in a third stage—applying his own initial and developing framework. In the normal course of listening, these three stages occur almost simultaneously; but we distinguish them to emphasize their separate importance, and particularly to highlight the first stage—the need to "listen" in its most literal sense, to take the role of the other. The scientific analysis can wait, possibly more advantageously, until long after the encounter. The second stage, like analysis, can wait too; but during the conversation, it does help to provide the researcher with meaningful probes.

Forms of Listening

Our model researcher must listen, then, to symbolic sounds to supplement and correct his observations. In the organizational and social movement situations in which he is involved, there is much talk; for building, or maintaining organization in the context of change, requires a great deal of talk. The hosts negotiate, argue, inform, and amuse each other; they plan, dream out loud, and reveal their organizational life even as they talk about external events which impinge upon it.

Eavesdropping

The researcher is well within earshot of this talk, so eavesdropping is a major source of actor-constructed information. Eavesdropping is natural; the researcher need not always elicit information—it is given both with and without awareness of his presence. Even overhearing only one end of a phone conversation can yield important findings. In this sense, listening to unsolicited sounds is functionally equivalent to watching the ongoing, existential scene of activity.

Eavesdropping is, of course, only one of several tactics for listening. Others include casual conversation on or off the scene, formal and informal interviewing. Theoretically, given enough time, the researcher will "hear it all" through eavesdropping and never have to resort to conversation or interview, although, of course, this is impractical.

There is an economic dimension to these different forms of listening. Eavesdropping has high cost-effectiveness early in field research and is much employed then, but thereafter its effectiveness diminishes, though never completely. At first, the researcher requires relatively little control over his "input" (except to prevent being "flooded"), since just about everything he hears is new data. As vocal events repeat themselves over and over, and as he asks questions about what he has casually overheard, other forms of talk take precedence: he begins to control the flow of verbal sound around him, economically and rationally directing it to his research purposes.

Situational conversation

Brief, situational or "incidental" questioning or conversation is extremely effective throughout the research; it is more controlled than eavesdropping and much less time-consuming for each unit of information gained. The researcher will resort to on-the-spot questioning when unsolicited verbalization as well as observations confound him. Asking questions is the simplest tactic in field research. Brief conversation is always economical, nothing is lost in its use unless the researcher has made a *faux pas;* hence, the researcher will use host-tactics which minimize asking the "wrong" question, at the "wrong" time, of the "wrong" person, in the "wrong" way. We can hardly detail this aspect of conversing beyond stating that the researcher is patient, polite, and cautious; he finds the natural way, and the opportunity for posing a question or two about what he has seen and heard. Asking questions can be perhaps the most important single tactic in field research except in the fully participant types of research, whether concealed or open.

Interviewing

There comes a time in the research when the lengthier interview is most effective because brief questioning, eavesdropping and casual conversation will only begin to answer important questions. The researcher now requires data on such matters as career, political or service ideology, and operational philosophy; and the lengthy interview is most economical for data gathering. Through the question-answer form, the interviewer can effectively control the flow of information. Early interviews tend to prove less economical than later ones, mainly because the researcher has not yet fully determined precisely what information he needs; also he is not always certain of what the respondent is telling him. This is why observation, eavesdropping, brief questioning, and casual conversation are so very important; they eventually provide a broad context for effective and economical interviewing.

At the site, the researcher regards all conversation between himself and others as forms of interviewing. Indeed, he would prefer to have most of his "interviews" this way, if possible; it is a natural way of getting information and a comfortable form of social engagement for him and for his hosts. The researcher finds innumerable occasions—on or off the scene, in elevators, hallways, lunch rooms, and even on the streets—to ask questions about things seen and heard, and about the informants themselves. The conversations may last only a few seconds or minutes, but they may lead to opportunities for lengthier sessions. The researcher creates, or seizes upon, the occasion for conversation and establishes a reasonable and comfortable stage for its development.

These lengthier—often relatively "private" or confidential—interviews are likely to take place in less public settings, such as offices or temporarily empty rooms or even at the interviewer's home. Such interviews can often be recorded on tape if necessary, and by agreement. When the conversation is less confidential and if there is no other place or time for it, then the researcher must create or seize opportunities for such interviews right out in public and despite potential interruptions caused by work or other activity.

Paradoxically, several decades ago the art and craft of conversation in social research was transformed into the formal "interview." This was necessitated by developments in survey research that required the standardization of interview topics (areas) and of questions and their wordings, and qualification of answers to process data gathered by many persons from a great many more persons.

But these properties of research are not particularly useful to the field researcher. He requires the variation and the nuance lost in questionnaire construction, and most of his respondents also require them for expressing their own actions and identities. Witness the annoyance, frustration—even fury—in a respondent's inability to express himself to his own satisfaction when confronted with questionnaire choices. Of course, the field researcher may playfully (in style) albeit seriously (in intent) use the forced-choice question, but respondents virtually always will insist on explaining why they chose one alternative rather than the other, or explain why they cannot. Those responses are exactly what the field researcher wished to elicit by his use of the technique.

The field researcher, then, regards the "interview" as a lengthy conversation. But its length, its probable prearrangement, and its frequent distance from the scene of action are no excuse for contrived formality in the interaction. Whatever it may be that the researcher is intent upon getting— a career sketch, statement of ideological position, an explanation of certain specific operations, or all of these—the researcher's mode approximates conversation. The way the researcher probes for detail, for clarity or explanation, and his gestures which signal normal surprise and even disbelief, provide him with the means for shaping an interview in this way. Of course, gestures are always judiciously controlled, but not significantly more or less than the situation seems to call for. A tactical error is made when the researcher smiles or laughs when the interviewee is dead serious; but equally is he in error when he fails to catch intended humor.

The researcher will expect to hear things he regards as "stupid" uttered in the name of cleverness, "evil" in the name of good. The kind of control he exercises is ordinary interpersonal tact, not control modeled after either survey research or nondirective therapy. Once the researcher has gained a measure of trust (probably in later conversations), he will be able even to taunt lightly or argue vigorously to elicit detail and find the respondent positively stimulated by the experience.

The interviewer does not use a specific, ordered list of questions or topics because this amount of formality would destroy the conversational style. He may have such a list in mind or actually in hand, but he is sufficiently flexible to order it in any way that seems natural to the respondent and to the interview situation. After all, what does one do when the respondent, while answering the first question, fully answers the third and some of questions six and seven? Far from becoming disorganized by this state of affairs, the interviewer builds upon what has apparently become a shared event. Conversation implies this very property.

But just as our researcher will not seek exclusive control over the interview process, he cannot allow the respondent to do that either. Here, he may have a "tug o' war" with the respondent, if the latter, however benignly, tries to run away with the interaction. To maintain a condition of balance in the conversation—where the interviewer does most of the leading and the respondent does most of the talking—the interviewer initially sets the stage for the interaction with a general statement which prepares (and implicitly coaches) the respondent for what is to follow: a substantive theme or a topical outline of several themes.

All this may be communicated in the opening moments of chit-chat, or while setting up a tape recorder. Even so, during the interview the respondent may not pick up important cues that plead for greater brevity per answer; some respondents are carried away by their own enthusiasm or vocal artistry, and speak as if starved for an audience. The researcher may have to take forceful steps; for example, gesture with his hands to attract attention, or study the respondent's breathing-talking rhythm to find the proper point for verbal intervention. On the other hand, control over the interview does not at all necessitate obvious maneuvers by the interviewer: depending on the nature of the evolving conversation, control may be appropriately exercised by a communications-sensitive respondent or requested by the respondent.

Interview Tactics

We can barely begin to tell of the many diverse forms the interview may take, particularly when the interviewer quite deliberately exercises only moderate control over its course. Every experienced interviewer will have a number of tactical measures for handling "difficult" respondents: ways of stimulating the inarticulate, loosening the tongue-tied, steering the "run-aways." (Some of the latter run in the direction of irrelevancies, while others become entangled in the minutia of relevancies.) All these require gestures tactically appropriate to the problem of hearing and listening: silence, facial expression, body movement, and a host of vocal gestures and questions that probe for such matters as chronology (. . . and then?; when was that?), detail (tell me more about that; that's very interesting), clarification (I don't quite understand; but you said earlier . . .), explanation (why?; how come?).

One of the fortunate properties of the interview regarded as conversation is that it need never appear to have a conclusion. Formal interviews have conclusions; but conversations, albeit intermittent, are like ordinary relationships, capable of continuity. However disappointing an interview may have seemed, it can be resumed at another time. For this reason, the researcher rarely concludes the interview with a simple "thank you, and goodbye"; he tells the respondent he has much to digest and think about, and that in this process he will probably find it necessary to call on him again (leaving his "thanks" implicit if that is more appropriate to the situation). Indeed, if in later examining the protocol, he does find food for thought, he would surely enhance his relationship with the respondent by finding an opportunity to tell him how valuable he found their conversation. The point is that a conversational interview, having been "suspended" rather than "terminated," can be comfortably activated again and again.

The novice, particularly, will find this property of interviews valuable for other reasons: the respondent's time unexpectedly may run out; or his own time, too, if he had unfortunately scheduled another interview for the time when this one was "just getting somewhere." And the novice will certainly have the experience of thinking he has gotten a great interview because "it went so well," only later to discover how little information he actually received. Then, he will know how valuable it was not to have terminated an interview. Seasoned field workers also occasionally get carried away by the mood of an interview and later discover—but with only temporary chagrin—that they mined less gold than lead.

The properties of continuity in relationships, informality, genuine interest, and courtesy, will probably leave the respondent pleased and even eager to be heard from again, particularly if he feels he has "performed well," and is not inordinately busy. Whatever the respondent's criteria for good performance, the researcher makes it possible for him to feel that way. *There is no more important tactic in this regard than to communicate the idea that the informant's views are acceptable and important.* And they *are,* whatever the interviewer as an ordinary person may believe; for as noted earlier he listens to "right" and "wrong" with equal equanimity and accepts what he hears at face value. For the interview at least, he is not therapist, evaluator, or investigator; he is a naturalist and his primary motives are to understand and to develop theory. This attitude and posture allows the informant to establish a relationship with the researcher that provides conditions for yielding ever more data.

Content comparability

Continuity in relationships has still another important function: providing conditions for building *comparability in content* to interviews he has had with other members of the same class of informant. This has implications for methodology generally, and for analysis in particular. The researcher may have in mind eventually to make intraclass and interclass comparisons on attitudes, commitment, roles, and the like. Initially, however, as we have seen he requires context and a feel for the ambience of the place; also, he is probably unprepared to standardize his questions because he does not know enough about these people to do so effectively. In studying a nascent social movement, he needs time to discover the significant classes, and time to form relationships. Thus, at first, our researcher is satisfied to regard the data obtained from interviews as a cumulative experience: the content of each interview or conversation gives form and substance to the next one. Indeed, if he were content to complete his study with only a general description, he would need to return to former respondents only as subsequent interviews suggested that the respondents were sources of information that was not given previously.

If the researcher plans to make comparisons among his respondents, he will soon begin to build content comparability into his interviews. But by that time he may be well along, and may have interviewed quite a few persons. Therefore, he returns to those persons interviewed earlier, perhaps with a more directed and shorter interview. More sophisticated now, he can efficiently get whatever information he needs from whomever he decides to interview. This is how he probably will do most of his research in the organizational setting.

In the case of the social movement, another problem exists: such movements tend to be geographically far-flung, and early informants often may be lost to follow-up interviews. Here, the researcher relies more upon the cumulative properties of the interview data than on their comparability; the data obtained from many of the early informants are "recycled"; that is, organized as a contextual mass rather than necessarily assigned to persons. Most of these interviews were probably rather sketchy anyway. But the experience gained in obtaining the information allows the researcher to develop a more comprehensive and pin-pointed interview schedule to use once he has discovered significant classes of adherents.

In either the organizational or social-movement settings, the researcher may decide to interview "formally" a series of persons. From each he seeks information bearing on approximately identical topics. The decision to carry out these particular interviews usually occurs well past the early stages of the research, after the researcher has developed hypotheses and propositions sufficiently important to be negated, verified or qualified via this lengthy, systematic series of interviews. Of course, many important propositions can be tested without doing such a series or even without any really "formal interview"—and many an excellent fieldwork study has been accomplished without them—but sometimes they are genuinely necessary. (One such instance involved testing several related propositions about the common-sense, rather than professional, "understandings" of psychotherapy held by nursing aides in a leading mental hospital.) [1] Two key points about such interviews, then, are that (1) they are done systematically rather than for exploratory or occasional purposes; and (2) they are carried out only when deemed necessary for checking upon the most important propositions developed during the research.

What does the interviewer actually wish of a would-be respondent? Of course, problems and interests vary, so we can hardly construct a single interview model that would satisfy all of them. Nevertheless we shall attempt one, bearing the following in mind: the researcher is a novice; while adept at asking specific questions in brief casual encounters, he is somewhat at a loss in sustaining, say an entire hour or more, with a key person in the organization; he wants to know a great many things about this person, and his relation to the organization.

Our more experienced researcher has a number of models symbolically tucked away—model interviews on career, ideology, institution, organization, work, and so on; he is rarely at a loss for a skeletal form for dialogue. In this instance, he is to have his first hour, his first organized encounter with a respondent, a health professional. He opts to use a career interview much in the form of a "tracer," which would also highlight the structure, purposes, and operations of the organization in and through which this career is unfolding. The model is quite lengthy; therefore, the interviewer will be selective, but he is also prepared to complete it over more than one such encounter.[2]

---

[1] Anselm Strauss et al., *Psychiatric Ideologies and Institutions* (New York: The Free Press, 1964; London: Collier-Macmillan Ltd., 1964).

[2] The model offered here is an exact copy of one which our students have been using successfully in their research training. It is designed most pointedly for shorter-term (1–2 months) field studies in psychiatric institutions with high density in the number of professionals. We include, as well, our comments and instructions to them. Generally, two or three students worked as a team with the labor divided among them.

The Health Professional Interview:
Career Model

Instructions to interviewers

In the short-term field study, we pay particular attention to the interview. It is a special mode of inquiry, particularly suited to the study of human beings, and quite necessary where the actions of people are either unfamiliar or very complex. While direct observation is the heart of field research, the interview must be used to provide context or meaning. Without this, much of the action seen appears as motion. Asking the actor what he is doing, and why, is a necessary corrective to unwarranted observer imputation and inference. We need him to tell us what it means to be a *professional* on a *career course,* working in an *institution,* with a *philosophy* (we assume) underlying his operations.

Our selected sample of would-be respondents covers every echelon, profession, major function, work shift, and seniority level. Hopefully, these represent the significant classes of person at the site. Still, as we interview, we will listen for classes we may have missed, so that representatives of these too may be sampled for interview purposes.

Bear in mind that fifty minutes is a clinician's special time reference. Unless the respondent indicates he is willing to talk for a longer period, it is best to schedule the unfinished portion of the interview for another time.

The interviewer will try to obtain relatively comparable coverage and content for each respondent; he will later analyze many interview protocols prepared by more than one interviewer. Nevertheless, each interviewer will use his own judgment on the order and manner in which he raises essential questions: also, take into account variability in interpersonal conduct according to the age, sex and status differential between interviewer and respondent. He may wish to proceed largely in chronological order; or he can elect to interview in terms of abstract categories such as treatment philosophy, professional roles, teamwork and institutional requirements. Following is a model which combines the two modes:

FACE SHEET DATA:

Father's occupation
Place of birth
Age
Ethnic identity, Religion
(If asking for these at the beginning appears too contrived wait until later, or at the end.)

CAREER:
  Pre-professional career alternatives
    (More natural to get "face data"
    here?)

Prior occupational choices, training, practice (fancied, planned, actual); considerations involved in their selection and abandonment; levels of commitment to them. (Back to high school and college.)

CAREER:
  Professional choice
  Prespecialization
    (prepsychiatric orientation, if
    any; for example, wanted first to
    be G.P. or research psychologist
    —never thought would specialize
    in psychiatry)

When and why first considered this profession (doctor, nurse, psychologist, social worker, occupational therapist); conditions for choice and strength of commitment: significant others as models; identifying own aptitudes and interests.

CAREER:
  Professional specialty

Choice point for psychiatric versus any other specialty (accidental, experimental, deliberate). How choice made (conditions, models). Early conceptions, images of work in that area.

IDEOLOGY, PHILOSOPHY:
  Prepractice

Very earliest conceptions of mental illness: etiology, prognosis, treatment and care; treatment preferences. Assessment of treatment efficacy for bulk of mentally ill, and for types in which he has special interest.

PROFESSIONAL TRAINING:
  Developing ideology
  Role models

Chronological listing of schools and in-service training institutions. Brief description of treatment philosophy at each; relate his developing ideology to each. What kinds of work tasks he was performing or seeing others perform (developing role concepts).

TEAMWORK:

Can begin here to probe for formative concepts of roles of other professional and para-professional types; imagery and estimates of these. Practice and perspectives on interprofessional teamwork.

CAREER: *Institutional choices*	Post training institutional work; where and why there? Probe for alternatives—searching for "right" place, refusals (own or institutional). Bring career to last point in time and place before present one; also ideological point.
CAREER: *Institution* *Professional work*	What brought him here? What did he know of this place in advance? What was he told and led to expect about the work he would do here?
INSTITUTION: *Ideology*	What did he know in advance, of the treatment style of this place, and its operational philosophy; also the limitations of the institution's requirements for the work he would be doing?
INSTITUTION: *Teamwork (interprofessional)*	First observations and impressions of his professional colleagues on all levels: what they did and what they claimed competence in. Did he accept or honor their practices and claims?
PROFESSION: *Institution*	Professional tasks when first came, and those which developed over time. Were these forced upon him, seized by him, proffered him? Rundown of daily, weekly tasks and responsibilities. What claims did he make, tacitly or forcefully? (Claims based on training, experience, tradition, legality, operational necessity, talent and desire.)
TEAMWORK: *Professional role* *Institution*	How do other personnel modify his work and his conception of what he ought to be doing? Of his tasks, which are done reluctantly, which positively? Which did he never dream he would be doing? Do this institution and his colleagues allow him to be the kind of professional he needs or wants to be?

IDEOLOGY:
  Profession

Currently, how does he define treatment? Who performs treatment? Then, how do the others figure ("merely" generally therapeutic)? Or is treatment the total milieu of the institution, or community participation? (Test for degrees of commitment or aversion to: one-to-one psychotherapy, small and large group therapies, therapeutic community, community psychiatry; also somatic therapies.)

INSTITUTION:
  Operational
  Operational philosophy

How does the respondent see operations: patient selection-rejection, admissions procedures, how patient progress is measured; transfer and discharge criteria and procedures? (From what perspective does he tell about these [rational-economics, particular treatment ideology, institutional efficiency, professional judgment]?)

CAREER:
  Profession
  Ideology
  Institution

Where does he see psychiatry going; what will it be like in 10–15 years? Treatment, institutional structure and operations?

What does he predict is the future of his profession, of other psychiatric professions: direction, training, work?

What does he predict for this institution in 10–15 years: its structure and operations?

What of himself? Would he dare predict, realistically and/or wistfully, where he will be in 10–15 years, and what he will be doing?

Additional Interviewing Tactics

In time, as relationships between researcher and hosts change, alterations in interview approach will change. At first, the researcher has been quite honestly naive, and accordingly most of his questions consisted of the reportorial type—who, what, when, where, and the how of events. In later stages, consistent with increasing sophistication and interpersonal familiarity and comfort, the researcher's questioning can be more "aggressive," to elicit new kinds of information. He may actually challenge assumptions and assertions made by his informants. We can list a number of challenging postures that the researcher may assume.

The Devil's Advocate Question. The field worker deliberately confronts the informant with the arguments of opponents as abstractions within or outside the universe being studied. By now, he has discerned variations in ideology or operational philosophy within the organization, and, taking the role of his informant's opponent, elicits rhetorical assertion. The data thereby obtained round out the observer's understanding of the informant's position and, not so incidentally, may test an emerging proposition bearing upon attitudinal differences within the organization or upon variations in commitment to the movement.

The Hypothetical Question. The interviewer uses still another technique for rounding out the informant's thought structure, but without the accompanying rhetorical heat. He poses a number of possible occurrences—for example, what if the effort to establish a branch of the organization in Chicago should fail? What if the patient committed suicide?

Posing the Ideal. Of this technique there are two variations. First, the informant is asked to describe the ideal situation, process, role or condition for achieving his or the organization's goals. Second, the interviewer himself poses an ideal, a construct developed from his experiences with the movement or organization, which pushes an observed process or role to its logical and desired extreme. In either instance what usually results is the generating of data by the comparison of an ideal with a "reality."

Offering Interpretations or Testing Propositions on Informants. It is sometimes very useful to tell informants—perhaps obliquely—about propositions that one is beginning to pull together. Such propositions may well challenge the understanding the informant has about what he or the organization is "really" up to. On the other hand, the researcher's understanding may also be challenged. This technique requires considerable courage on the part of the researcher, but its payoff for validation and for new data are immense. The sequence is familiar enough: the researcher poses a proposition, and then asks the informant how the idea squares with his understanding of some situation, condition, process or relationship.

The response can go one of two ways:

(1) The researcher is told—one way or the other—that he simply does not understand, partially or completely. He then asks (as a learner) what is wrong with the proposition. After being told, he has new or additional data, and he makes his own judgment as to how the informant's critiques

and evidence bear upon his proposition, or upon any other proposition. For example, the counter-assertion may reflect the position of the informant in the organization or may reflect his ideology, and not really invalidate the proposition. But it may invalidate it, or "force" a decisive change in its formulation. In either case the researcher has gained something—knowledge and perhaps even some humility.

(2) The researcher is told that his formulation is correct, or better still, that the informant had "never thought of it that way." Here the researcher gets a measure of validation, and makes something of a contribution to someone's understanding of himself, of his group, and of their collective experience.

The number of such tactics that can be used to gain verbal information is practically limitless. There are, however, two especially effective ones which bear mention. First, *group interviews* can be arranged beforehand, or arise spontaneously and involve established or casual groupings. Consider this natural sequence: the researcher is observing several persons perform a number of related tasks; he makes a comment to, or questions, one of the hosts. Another eavesdropping host joins in the conversation—and then, perhaps, another and another. Soon there is animated discussion; a group interview is in process even as the various hosts continue their normal activity.

However it is established, the group interview telescopes some aspects of a series of one-to-one interviews. (It is, in fact, one type of "multiple-respondent" interview; others consist of conversations with two, three, or more respondents in either formal or informal interview situations, where relationships among respondents can be quite complex and their views diverse.) In addition, this form of information gathering provides an especially nice situation for revealing variations in perspective and attitude, and a ready means, through subtle pitting of one against the other, for distinguishing between shared and variable perspectives. The pitting process hardly needs manipulation, since the hosts themselves, by speech and gesture, will naturally "correct" each other's rendering of "reality." By contrast, in the one-to-one interview the pitting is more calculated, and probably is without any immediate corrective for the respondent.

For the researcher, of course, everything he sees and hears is "corrective" of everything else he sees and hears. Nevertheless, in and through the group interview, the researcher has expressed his interest in the hosts, exhibited his desire to listen and learn, learned some new things—including a general sense of what he does not know. He has also developed a natural opportunity for requesting further information—this time individually from only those in the group whose contribution would bear most directly on something of theoretical importance. While one-to-one interviews have certain advantages, the researcher eagerly creates or seizes opportunities for group and multiple respondent interviews.

A second tactic, that of *"tracing"* involves following a single person on his normal tour of activities throughout a given period of time—hours or even days. This tactic is modeled on the tracer used in physiological research whose movements through the body and effects upon tissue highlight biological process. In social research, the human subject as tracer analogously fosters the discovery and understanding of properties both of social structure and organizational process. This tactic is most effective when the person occupies a position that cuts across several jurisdictions, or when his activities constitute processes that affect most of the organization. (Novitiates undergoing early socialization in service institutions or in social movements make good tracers because often they are not yet securely located in a single jurisdictional area; also selected patient or client types that filter through service institutions provide an especially enlightening perspective on such institutions.)

Through his sampling procedure or on-the-spot decisions based on observation, the researcher makes his selections of tracers. He chooses few, since these tracer tactics are costly in the expenditure of time. Once having gained the cooperation of a subject, the researcher explains the procedure and coaches the subject. The procedure is simple enough: the person is asked to tell and explain what he is doing, going to do or has just done— the choice depends on whichever is most convenient or feasible.

For many persons, this experience of being followed through a series of activities is delightful and flattering, for others it may create apprehension over appearances and performance; but if done voluntarily, it usually turns out well for the observer, since he gets somewhat different data bearing on work or life process. An additional dividend is that, if not too busy, "the tracer" will pause now and then to give what amounts to informal interviews, as well as commentaries on people whom he encounters as he moves around. However, if he is so preoccupied with his work that he cannot even pause to explain very much of its meaning, he can still be interviewed afterward. So can the persons with whom he has interacted that day as he moved about.

Interviews: Contingencies and Forms

Despite preceding discussions of frequently useful tactics and our suggestive model for a formal interview, it should be well understood that there can be no cookbook recipes for interviewing. Those would be more crippling than helpful, and anyhow they would scarcely be adaptable to the enormous range of conversations that go by the name of interviews. To plan on and guide specific kinds of conversations, it is essential that the researcher be able to think in terms of an array of contingencies that may affect the content of a given interview (or have affected one recently completed), as well as how those contingencies may affect (or have affected) the form of an interview.

Expected duration

Expected duration is among the most important of contingencies. Will the interview last only a few minutes, an hour, several hours? Does it take place at a place and time that will limit its duration, or can it be extended a bit or for many additional minutes, either because the respondent is persuaded to continue talking or because he is so enjoying the conversation? Short duration limits not only the conversational territory that can be covered but affects the tactics which the interviewer is likely to use, such as the leisurely exploration of conversational byways, the permitting of digressions, and the exchanging of views so as to obtain additional information. Interviews of long duration allow the interviewer to prolong the conversation, delaying its final moments with subtle tactics if necessary, including the closing of his notebook (or stopping the taping) but thereafter delaying for a few last conversational exchanges that often yield important bits of extra information. Longer interviews also allow the interviewer to ease slowly and often sociably into the heart of the interview; if neither he nor the respondent know each other too well, there is time to "feel each other out."

Single interviews versus series

Another important contingency is whether this is a one-shot interview or one of several, and where in that series it falls. If it is the first of an expected series of meetings, then the interviewer may be more concerned with building good relationships than with getting good information, and his tactics will be appropriate to that end. If both persons have conversed many times—whether in formal or informal interviews—then the current one will be much affected by that history. Thus, after many informal talks, if the interviewer wishes to have a "formal" interview, complete with its recording on tape, he has to figure out how to carry on that more formal conversation without violating the spirit and the forms of previous conversations.

Setting

Still another contingency consists of the setting within which the interview occurs. Conversation that is appropriate to the private office is inappropriate to a crowded lunchroom; likewise, topics can be broached that fit in naturally with the normal flow of coffee-time conversations regardless of the expected duration of the coffee break. Appropriate conversation implies not only proper topics but proper style of speech, gesture, modes of address and types of interplay (joking, banter, or daily exchange of gossip or other information).

Identities

Another class of contingency consists of the various relevant identities of the conversationalists. Is the interviewer regarded as something of an outsider (as certainly he is early in most studies)? Is he knowledgeable, and does he show his knowledge, about many of the events which occur at this locale because he has had experiences like them before? Likewise is the respondent an old-timer or a relative new-comer? (Eventually the interviewer will have "been around" much longer than some newly arrived members of the social movement or the organization.)

Along other identity dimensions, what are the interviewer's and respondent's respective sexes? Ages? Social class positions? All those are likely to affect the course of an interview, whether *in toto* or in part. Sex differences may "naturally" inhibit, but they may also allow more expression to certain views and actions: the interviewer can deliberately play upon the other's femininity or his own masculinity—or he may do well to suppress that aspect of himself.

The same is true of class differences: For instance, the interviewer may have to mute that difference and underline respective *similarities* of identity, or emphasize their shared situational identities (both have just witnessed an important event that both need to talk about or would enjoy discussing). Other important identities are whether the respondent regards himself as an expert or "just ordinary," or a leader or a "marginal" person in the organization; also whether the respondent initiated the interview or merely granted the interview.

Interviews tend to be organized around one or more such dimensions of identity, whether so designed by the interviewer or not. Yet, even relatively short conversations may have several component phases, each organized around somewhat different dimensions, or clusters of dimensions of identity. Thus, learner–teacher relations may govern some phases but age similarities or sex differences may more greatly affect other phases. And the interviewer may maneuver the conversation from one dimension to another, depending on his own purposes.

Respondent styles

Consider, also, contingencies presented by variations in the "interpersonal styles" of respondents. The latter are variously shy or bold, quick or slow, casual or formal, direct and concrete or subtle and abstract. These and other attributes of persons will surely give shape to the process or the interview as a career—to the approach, the engagement, and the disengagement. Finally, respondents will vary greatly in the kind and degree of their commitment to their work and to their work identities: one respondent may be "deeply involved" in and "dead serious" about the very things the researcher wants to question him on; the next respondent, distanced by humor or cynicism, may playfully "field" each question. Since researchers, too, have variable style and commitment—and variable abilities to handle this variety in others—we have the makings of an almost infinite number of conversational forms.

The contingencies noted above are only a few among many possible ones which affect interaction during interviews. That interaction—including the calculated tactics of the interviewer, and quite possibly the interactional tactics of the respondent—is what gives the conversation its form. By "form" we mean such characteristics as length; rate of speech, and interchange (including number and length of silences); the length of periods of preliminary and closing interchanges; the relative amounts of talking by each participant during various phases of the interview; the percentage of remarks couched as questions and who asks them; who actually controls various phases of the conversation; who gives the signals marking termination of the interview; how the interview is actually closed off; and, in general, the "tone" of the entire conversation.

The experienced interviewer tends during each interview to be aware of its particular characteristics and to be alert to why those characteristics are appearing. (Of course, he helps to make some of them appear through his deliberate, if ad hoc, tactics.) In one-shot interviews, it is especially important that he recognize what is transpiring and why. For repeated interviews, he need not be quite so alert or inventively tactical, because if not satisfied with the course taken by a given interview, and with the information yielded by it, he can always attempt to analyze "where it went wrong." Nevertheless, it is immensely important that the interviewer learn to think of his interviews in terms of "contingencies" and "forms."

We say contingencies and forms rather than determining contingencies and resulting forms, because sometimes the specifically evolving interview allows the interviewer to use or invent tactics which change the contingencies—such as stretching the length of a prearranged interview or suggesting "let's move to a quieter place."

In sum: It is much more important to think structurally (contingencies and forms) about conversations than to memorize—or even capitalize on —set arrays or repertoires of conversational tactics. We might add that this kind of interview analysis is even more important for the fieldworker than for most other kinds of researchers, because it feeds back directly into his analysis of the field situation and of the events taking place within the field. Luckily for him and for his ultimate understanding of his data, exactly the reverse analytic process (from understanding the field to understanding the interview) also takes place. That is one of the great advantages of field research.

The Host as "Strategic" Informant

Thus far in this chapter we have depicted the researcher as an active seeker after information, an initiator of interaction and someone who utilizes a variety of tactics. Yet, special devices for actively engaging people are not always necessary. As the hosts come to accept the researcher's presence, they will approach him almost as much as he will them, and to give as well as to get information.

Consider how the hosts might size up the situation: the researcher is someone whose work consists in comprehending "us," including "me" and my work; he will soon tell us all something of what he has found, and eventually he will make all his findings public to everyone. One host may ask, "Why didn't he interview me?" Another, "I wonder whether he really understood what I told him?" Any or all may ask, "What are the others telling him? What is he really after?" Considering that those who are observed may feel that their perspectives, statuses, or personal interpretations of events are underrepresented or misunderstood, the research situation from their perspectives may present an unsettling condition. After all, the observed are observers too, and they too have "data" that tell them that the researcher has possibly been watching the "wrong" things, listening to such "questionable sources" as unhappy clients or even to colleagues who stand in positions structurally or ideologically opposed to themselves.

Therefore, the researcher can expect his hosts to attempt getting their messages across to him. They, too, need not always use special devices; for example, they can and probably do exert control over the researcher's eavesdropping as well as manage to "inform" him during the ordinary course of conversations and lengthy interviews. In the eavesdropping situation, discussions and even arguments occasionally will occur precisely because the researcher is present; the situation becomes a ready-made stage for communicating a thought, a mood, a definition. These messages are no less authentic because the researcher is there to hear them. The researcher will judge this talk just as he judges anything else that he hears—against what he has seen or heard at other times, and in other contexts. Messages given by "insiders" provide different data or finer distinctions among events than he, as an "outsider," could hope to get in other ways. He welcomes them because actor-constructed realities constitute most of his data.

The hosts, then, can control somewhat the eavesdropping, the casual conversation, and the planned interview to get their views across. Yet, for some even this is not enough. Perhaps their relationships to the organization plus the presence of a professional listener add up to a unique and compelling situation. The disgruntled, the frustrated, the enthusiasts—in fact, theoretically anyone other than an uncommitted jobholder—may be concerned lest the researcher not "get it right." These persons may opt to provide the "truth" privately. Why not always in the ordinary course of an interview?

Frequently, the interviewer is too intent upon getting what *he* wants rather than what the respondent most wants to talk about, for some respondents play their roles too well and allow the interviewer to control the relationship. Also, some interviews are done early in the research before some respondents have developed much trust; or the interview itself so stimulates the respondent that for days afterwards he tells himself what he should have said, and then he believes that he needs another opportunity to talk. Whatever the reason, the researcher can expect frequently to hear someone say, especially when nobody else is nearby, "Let me tell you what really goes on around here," or simply, "You should have been here this morning," as a preliminary signal either for a "unique" perspective or a "juicy" vignette about something deemed important to the researcher from the projected view of the host. Aside from anticipating new data, the researcher can now feel he is part of the general flow of activity, that his presence is catalytic in providing him with the symbolic representations of reality he needs.

The Interviewer as Strategic Informant

Understandably, the researcher also is sought out to tell what he knows. The same condition that impels the host to cue the researcher may cause him to question the researcher about just what it is he is "finding" or had "found." "I'm dying to know," or "I can't wait until you give us your report," are frequent exclamations. These indicate impatience or concern over appearances, and less usually mere curiosity, since identities are at stake and the value of work and commitment are subject to question. For several basic reasons, the researcher is most careful about what he tells anyone: He dare not betray information given in confidence; for a considerable period of time, he knows too little about the scene or has too little confidence in his "knowledge"; information gained from him, a neutral observer, provides potent ammunition for internal conflicts. The researcher knows that almost from the very start of the research he may have to ward off those who want "tips," conclusions, impressions, and the like. He cannot readily ignore or rudely refuse requests for information; good social relations are a major instrument in his work.

"Begging off"

In anticipation of requests for information, particularly when these imply private communication, the researcher is prepared to use a number of tactics. First, he simply "begs off": he honestly indicates that "it is too early"; he does not know enough; he is just beginning to understand; he needs much more information before he can say anything that might be both valid and valuable. He gets the questioner to take his role, to "see" how difficult it must be for an outsider to learn a great deal in so short a time.

Also, he can hark back to a pledge he had made earlier to the effect that he will have something of value to say to everyone towards the end of his work. The "begging off" tactic usually works well enough early in the research. While it yields nothing to the questioner, it does not insult him. The point about insult is especially noteworthy: since reciprocity is so integral to human relationships is it not natural that information flow two ways? The researcher bears in mind that a very fine line exists between being an informant and being an intellectual colleague. If he does not think so, the informant may.

Forestalling

Sometimes "begging off" may not be feasible, particularly when one or more hosts are persistent. Their demand for participation by everyone, consistent with the roles being played, applies to the researcher as well as to everyone else. He recognizes this as natural and, as we have indicated earlier, his behavior should be natural to his role. Hence, his second tactic is to forestall. From the outset, he has been making comments appropriate to what he is watching or listening to: he appears to be (and is) a participant. In the company of others he is not constantly unresponsive. If nothing else, he is asking questions that "tell" where his interests lie; and how he asks them cues his listeners to the logic of his thinking. Also, his nonvocal gestures of humor, concern, fascination, and general warmth attest to his participation and provide information of a sort. Of course, for some hosts this is not enough.

Giving "bits" of information

Still another tactic is to provide "information bits." The researcher severely controls his "output" but attempts to satisfy his questioners. After all, he has enormous amounts of data, and though most are undigested, he can find some facts and make some inferences that meet the requirements of actual or potential questioners but in no way compromise his research or the persons or the organization. This tactic is scarcely distinguishable by them from ordinary chatter or commentary; for example, there has been an argument and some confusion at a meeting attended by the researcher, and one of the hosts turns to him and asks, "What must a sociologist be thinking about such a disorganized group?" The observer may answer, "That doesn't necessarily mean 'disorganization'; all groups express differences from time to time. It shows you are alive and growing, and that there is the freedom and equality which allows for the expression of differences."

Alternatively, picking up on contemporary values, he may answer by asking another question: "Would you want to work in an organization where all rules and roles are set from above?" The researcher can always prepare a number of "disposable" items—comments about people and activities that satisfy the requirements of sociability—and avoid revealing sensitive or unsupported materials. He may express surprise that there are so many of this or so few of that or exclaim that he had never realized something or other.

Curiously—and most important—though the comments may not satisfy the questioner, they often actually serve to elicit countercomment; that is, they convert the questioner into an informant. Nevertheless, the information bits are numerous enough to satisfy almost any host: support for the unhappy, sympathetic explanation for the disgruntled, praising statements for the enthusiasts. Most social situations provide properties or qualities that are humorous, chidable, redemptive, praiseworthy, and just plain interesting. The researcher surely need not always accept straightforwardly attempts by others to cast him into an informant role.

Reporting

Finally, there is the tactic of "reporting," of giving the specified action that most legitimately and fully meets the explicit contract of reciprocity between researcher and the hosts. Here, the researcher is on relatively safe, if not always comfortable, grounds: Perhaps it is late in the research, and he has many analytic memos, the credibility of which will allow him to perform intelligently and with some distinction in public. By now, he knows his hosts quite well; their questions and statements have long since signalled their expectations of him. He "owes" them, and can provide, a statement that is lucid and relevant to them. In some measure, of course, he may disappoint his audience—not because he has so little of substance to say, but because his orientation and developing perspective perhaps have led him in directions of lesser interest to his hosts. Still, he has much data and has thought a good deal about them, and can prepare something of value even while he may be thinking of other audiences. What, then, does he tell his listeners, and how does he present his report?

The report takes some courage to give, but giving it need not be an ordeal if the researcher "sets a good stage"—a tactic that gets his listeners to take his role as an observer of their scene. He reveals his framework and his interests; for what he wants them to hear is not only substance that is of interest from the hosts' perspectives, but the "same" substance understood in the context of *his* perspective. His value to them will rest on whatever new perspective and understandings he can impart, certainly not merely on the support of existing perspectives, which may themselves be formed out of commitments to ideology to the movement, institution,— or worse still—out of platitudes and clichés.

Therefore, though he offers those propositions that he anticipates will be understandable and meaningful, they are sociologically oriented, grounded, and analytically rendered. This is precisely where the "payoff" lies in return for the observer's having maintained his conceptual distance. This same distance will have helped him to determine which of his many propositions and concepts will be most appropriate and meaningful to his audience. The selection may bear upon roles, the division of labor, leadership—in fact, anything of sociological significance.

Nor does the researcher as informant overly concern himself with saying only nice things about his hosts and their activities. Now his own honesty, integrity and intelligence are subject to question; therefore his concern is with cogency, significance, and validity. The researcher is not narrowly judgmental nor critical: his interpretation of the hosts' world and their activities is judicious, therefore probably educational; it is appreciated on these counts alone. This is what he finally does—perhaps it is all he *can* do, short of telling them what he may believe they should really be doing. Quite probably if his report is cogent, the researcher will have wisely provided his hosts with a kind of mirror, which may well prove to be enough of a response.

Suggested Reading

Most writing on listening is organized around the concepts of communications (including the nonverbal) and interviewing. However titled, the following items reflect closely many of the ideas presented in this chapter. Two good books on the subject are:

GORDON, RAYMOND L., *Interviewing Strategy, Techniques and Tactics.* Homewood, Ill.: The Dorsey Press, 1969.
An extensive discussion of interviewing covering major facets of the art and craft of gaining information for research purposes. Many very practical models for approaching and engaging others for these purposes are provided, as is an extensive bibliography.

RICHARDSON, STEPHEN A., BARBARA S. DOHRENWEND, and D. KLEIN, *Interviewing, Its Forms and Functions.* New York: Basic Books, Inc., 1965.
A good general discussion of the structures and strategies of interviewing.

Some general articles or book chapters include:

BECKER, HOWARD S., and BLANCHE GEER, "Participant Observation and Interviewing: A Comparison," *Human Organization,* XVI, No. 3 (1957), 28–32; also in McCall-Simmons, *Issues in Participant Observation: A Text and Reader.* Reading, Mass.: Addison-Wesley Publishing Co., 1969; and in William J. Filstead, *Qualitative Methodology: Firsthand Involvement with the Social World.* Chicago: Markham Publishing Company, 1970.
Strongly supports the proposition that interviewing alone will not assure the field researcher the necessary information that he requires to make valid inferences.

DEAN, JOHN P., ROBERT L. EICHORN, and LOIS R. DEAN, "Observation and Interviewing," in John T. Doby, *An Introduction to Social Research* (2nd ed.), pp. 274–304. Des Moines, Iowa: Meredith Corporation, 1967. Also in McCall-Simmons, *Issues in Participant Observation.*
Offers useful taxonomy of respondent types, suggesting that different kinds and amounts of data relate to respondent position, attitude, and general background; see especially pp. 384–86.

PAUL, BENJAMIN D., "Interviewing Techniques and Field Relations," in A. C. Kroeber et al. (ed.), *Anthropology Today: An Encyclopedic Inventory,* pp. 430–51. Chicago: University of Chicago Press, 1953.

Excellent article which illustrates how interviewing is done in the field context—a great deal of it "informally."

WHYTE, WILLIAM F., "Interviewing in Field Research," in R. N. Adams and J. J. Preiss (eds.), *Human Organization Research,* Chapter XXVII, pp. 352–74. Homewood, Ill.: The Dorsey Press, 1960.

Very informative discussion of structure and process in interviewing with helpful suggestions for the interviewer on how to pose questions and evaluate answers.

The following articles show interviewers facing different problems when interviewing in distinctive field situations:

BECKER, HOWARD S., "Interviewing Medical Students," *American Journal of Sociology,* LXII (1956), 199–201.

LEZNOFF, M., "Interviewing Homosexuals," *American Journal of Sociology,* LXII (1956), 202–4.

VAN HOFFMAN, N., and S. W. CASSIDY, "Interviewing Negro Pentecostals," *American Journal of Sociology,* LXII (1956), 195–97.

6

Strategy for Recording

To exercise maximum control over his experiences, the researcher requires an efficient system for recording them. Novices may think of note-taking and recording principally as devices that help with remembering and with the storage and retrieval of information. They are correct, but only on a rather mechanical level. Therefore, the problems of merely remembering and storing information are not central to our theme in this chapter. What our researcher requires are recording tactics that will provide him with an ongoing, developmental dialogue between his roles as discoverer and as social analyst. This is our central theme. Before developing it, we would say of the "remembering problem" only that memory improves considerably in its use; field researchers have learned this, often to their own amazement. Our observer knows this and will make adjustments, particularly to his early disappointments over the possible shallowness of his "ready recall."

Taking Notes

To discuss recording, we must go back to the beginning of the researcher's study. From the very outset of his visits to a potential research site—and certainly after coming away from the first visit, having made some entrée statement—the researcher will have gathered considerable data. These data are in the form of observations and impressions. In short order— after a bare few minutes, in fact—the researcher is "threatened" with a crush of observations and interpretations, and he must quickly attend to the problem of recording. It will not do simply to write notes on little slips of paper to be sorted out much later. For the long haul, the researcher needs a more sophisticated system. Initially, this sorting problem, as well as the remembering problem, necessitates systematic recording tactics. Later it becomes clear that a reliable set of data are necessary for other reasons— principally to provide a fund of everlastingly fresh and potentially genera- tive data for systematic analysis; also, to maintain control over operational decisions which bear upon observational selection, timing and sequencing.

To show how our model researcher will begin to do his recording sys- tematically, let us construct a typical situation wherein he has scheduled for himself approximately one hour of observation at a new site or sub-site. He will stay awhile, perhaps converse with a few persons, and take some notes. His expectations are simple enough: to come away with a few vignettes, many indicative verbal fragments, and a number of general im- pressions. (Rather than discuss here what it might be the researcher is looking at or for, we refer the reader back to our discussions on selective sampling and the grounds for watching. These plus the notion of a "passing parade" of events will provide the imagery necessary to take the research- er's role.)

If the observer's identity and general purposes are known and more or less accepted, perhaps he may take notes in the presence of others without significantly altering the scene; note-taking is a common enough occur- rence and certainly in keeping with the research role. Still, there will be times when it is inappropriate to do so: for example, in the midst of a heated argument or during a solemn occasion. The researcher will cer- tainly not carry a clipboard with many sheets of paper and write copiously! He may, however, leave the scene briefly to write notes—a tactic that may also serve to give the hosts some relief from "surveillance."

Whatever the decision, his notes will be very brief—mere words, phrases, possibly a drawing. Their purpose is to provide stimulation for recall done within a matter of hours. A single word, even one merely descriptive of the dress of a person, or a particular word uttered by someone usually is enough to "trip off" a string of images that afford substantial reconstruc- tion of the observed scene. If the scene is productive, and the note-taking not at all disturbing, the researcher possibly will decide to remain longer. The notes are giving him some comfort because they seem to dam up a moderate tide of data.

However, sometimes there is a veritable flood—that is, the observer feels bursting with ideas about what he is witnessing and inundated with sight and sound. Here, he must calculate the value of the ideas against that of new data. He must decide whether to stay, hoping he will later recall his imagery, or to leave in order to save his ideas although he will lose some data. For the experienced observer, unless he is quite tired, this is not a major crisis: he will probably not forget his ideas; also, at another time he can expect to see much the same action.

A more important decision awaits him at the end of his allotted hour of observation. If it is to be his last for the day, then he can wait for several hours before processing his notes. However, if it is to be followed by an interview or another hour of observation elsewhere, then he will have to determine whether his notes will stand the test of memory. He needs to "unload" his experiences so that he may view the next scene refreshed, almost as if for the first time. His notes are rather spare and many hours will pass before he gets to type or tape them. They begin to lose value uncomfortably soon. Hence, if possible, the experienced researcher provides himself with an interlude and a measure of seclusion for note-processing to increase their longevity. To the original notes he adds contextual properties, some reflections, and perhaps additional quotable material. Now, the notes will "last" for one or two days, after which again they rapidly begin to lose value. What the researcher wishes very much to avoid is the common experience of having a pocketful of barely legible and hardly understandable notes. Later in the research, as scenic properties become relatively repetitious, holding data in mind becomes far less burdensome. Even the unprocessed spare notes will hold better.

Typing or taping?

Still, even with processed notes of relatively good quality, the researcher must concern himself with another stage of processing: typing or taping. Just as important, however, is that he has still not fully "heard himself" think about what he has witnessed. He knows that while writing not only will he state the "facts," but he will create meanings and realities. These must be handled relatively soon after the actual observations. Still other decisions press in on him early in the research (unless through long experience he has developed a total system of recording): how to process days and days of similar notes; how much detail and coverage are necessary for current and later analysis; indeed, whether to tape the notes and have them transcribed by someone else, or to type them himself, and whether on cards or paper. More important, perhaps, are the problems of categorically ordering or chronologically sequencing the multitude of items on his note pad.

Just a brief word about taping and typing: The temptation to dictate one's notes onto tape is considerable, particularly if money is available for transcribing them. With a little practice in front of the tape recorder, data, impressions, and interpretations easily tumble out one after the other. An hour of observation and thought can be unloaded in less than twice that time. Also, if the researcher is part of a research team, often there is a great advantage to telling teammates about his latest observations. He gets the observations while they are very fresh "down on tape," simultaneously he keeps his colleagues abreast of "the latest." An audience helps also to speed up and make vivid the relating of the account.

However, there are counterbalancing disadvantages: the transcriber soon has a huge backlog of tapes, perhaps cannot hear them too well, fails to make suitable paragraphing, does not get the work done (perhaps even quits the job) until many days later. Also, the danger of losing control over the entire recording process is considerably increased with the use of tapes, if only because weeks may pass before the observer has access to the transcribed notes, and because probably their actual arrangement on paper does not readily lend itself to efficient retrieval of information. Then, what of typing? Here, control is better but one must spend much more time at the typing than at the dictating process.

However the notes are recorded, whether by taping or typing (or a combination), the *ordering of data* looms as a special problem. After weeks or months of recording a veritable mountain of experience, the amount and continuous flow of data may threaten the researcher almost as much as did the original experience. He performs little service for himself when he simply pours out his relatively scattered torrent of observations and thoughts, with little more concern for later work than the simple dating of materials. His eventual search for a specific datum, or for an "idle thought" later recognized as important, threatens him with time wasted and tedium —unless when recording he has prepared his notes according to the future dialogue with himself.

Generally, the notes are a very private production, to be shared during the course of the study only with research team mates. Later, following the study, when other purposes and interests develop, the record may be shared with other colleagues and even perhaps with graduate students for teaching purposes. The researcher bears very much in mind, however, that the documents contain confidential information on what trusting persons have said and done; he is very much obligated to respect that trust and, when necessary, to mask the identities of those persons. But there is a very positive function to be found in the privacy of these documents. Privacy allows the researcher the nearly absolute freedom to render his experiences and interpretations exactly as he wishes. Privacy grants him license to interpret, infer, conjecture, or pursue any creative impulse in thought, including those that later prove to be quite ridiculous.

Shortly, we will show how this also can be done in ways quite independent of the recording of events as originally experienced. We would only repeat what was said earlier: that substantive understanding and methodological operations are created in the research process, and that experience itself will, with continued recording and examination, provide the necessary corrective for any error of interpretation or reasoning.

These final notes of the researcher are prepared so that they will stand the test of time: that is, be legible and understandable for months or years to come. They include enough detail, context (including time and place), and subtleties to recreate the observed situation and the thoughts and feelings that these once provoked in him. The document remains a relatively permanent fund of experience, as original and as complete as his time and patience will allow.

The model that we shall now depict as any other field work record, is geared to "instant" as well as developmental and "final" analysis. A good set of notes quickly becomes a "constant companion"—a sort of alter ego composed of factual and reliable data, a running account of fleeting and developed interpretations and reflections, and a chronicle of operational decisions made at stated times, places, and circumstances. The recording grows even as the recorder does; yet, it is a more stable and reliable repository of "fresh" experience, including observations and thoughts about them, than is the recorder himself. The record can be regarded, once it is well along in its development, as confronting the recorder during different stages in his own development. Therein lies an important interactional process through which the researcher discovers new properties in scenes and in relationships hitherto unnoticed though "recorded," and through which he will, hopefully, develop concepts and propositions about the nature of the scene.

The recording also will exert considerable control over the discovery process; it will offer negative, conflicting, or supporting evidence, and it will warn of insufficient evidence, thereby "demanding" new or further observations. Although the researcher surely can get help and corrections from teammates or other colleagues, or from his reading, the "companion" has the advantage of being always available and reliable and often more helpful.

Of course, each researcher will develop a recording system that reflects himself and one which, whatever its shortcomings, will facilitate his productivity. We would not presume to tell readers how to do it, particularly if they already have systems and are comfortable with them. For those in search of a system, however, we offer the one that our model researcher uses. We do this, not only to show "how to . . . ," but to reveal some significant properties of field research that are reflected in recording activity, regardless of its form. Our intent is to show that recording is central to every aspect of the research endeavor.

The Model

Whether he types his notes or talks them into tape, the researcher organizes them in relatively distinct "packages" of material according to whether they constitute "Observational Notes" (ON), "Theoretical Notes" (TN), or "Methodological Notes" (MN). Two consecutive pages of actual, undoctored field notes follow. They were taken from a larger set of notes made during a six-week study (early 1960s) of a county psychiatric inpatient unit. Quite deliberately, we selected a segment that reveals more about the researcher and his field-noting than about his object of study.

ON: Asked the tech "what kinds of patients do you usually get on the ward?" "Mainly schizy ones" she says, then proceeded to categorize them by sex and age. But most of her answer contained a string of categories more descriptive of behavior or personality: "angry ones," "noisy," "withdrawn," and "real crazy ones." Then, without my asking, she said: "You have to control them or they give you a hard time."

ON: I asked her what she meant by schizy? Said: "you know, crazy." I asked her if she'd be able to tell if a person were schizy—if the doctor or nurse had not told her, or if the person were on the street in her line of sight? Her answer was: "Sure, you'd be able to tell if they were mumbling to themselves or if they were bothering people."

ON: The above conversation went on, covering things I can't recall now (tho nothing particularly noteworthy it seems). But then I pointed to several patients and asked her to tell me about the one she knew best. "That one has been here several times this year." I pursued this, and what I got from her was the idea that some patients are in and out of the hospital several times "for years." I asked how come? She said she didn't know but that they "sure get to act like they belong here," and later added, "they sometimes get to know more about psychiatry than is good for them."

TN: This tells us a little more about how the techs think; about their level of thinking relative to the pros. But we can't say all the techs think this way (see Monday's notes, Nov. 15, on the conversation with the tech who is a college grad). Maybe can classify the techs on levels of comprehension? Is this worth a memo? Right now it doesn't excite me.

MN: It seems like for days I've been piling up a fair number of ideas, but none recently really grabs me. I'll prepare a list of these and review them to see which warrants pursuing.

TN: There's one idea implicit above—on pts who keep coming back and who get to feel at home—which strikes me as important as well as interesting: Some patients may become professional, qua patient, and learn, as in a residency training program, the ways of success in patienthood: the lingo, roles, attitudes, etc. Maybe makes for fine counter-roles to the legitimate pros. Is this what staff mean when they talk of "fostering dependency?"

MN: Arrange chat with chief and head nurse. Probe for meaning of dependency—not as passive consequence of hospital stay but as active, positive means on part of patient to make a career; maybe these patients find a psychiatric career—albeit as patient—more attractive than any other right now. Interview a few of the old-timers among patients.

TN: This stimulates another thought: (see notes of Nov. 10th on discharge meeting—the argument over whether George be kept or discharged). Maybe the only way to run a therapeutic community is to select or keep only those patients who make the community a success. Maybe there is a sort of "calculus of patienthood" where the patient has to get a certain high score to be retained for the longer term, and those who fail to, get shipped out. Does a hospital, with residency training, also have a calculus but use a different numerical system so that residents can get better (appropriate to 1–1 psychotherapy) practice ? Or more pleasant, or with better chances of success? After all, why deal with a 50 yr. old, obese, ugly, chronically depressed woman?

MN: It all sounds kinda cynical but the more I think about those patients who are kept and those shipped off to state hosp., the more valid it seems. So: 1. scan all data to date for evidence on both professional patient and calculus; 2. interview chief, social worker, head nurse; 3. prepare memo if either or both pan out. Maybe link both concepts around "mutual selection process."

ON: Observational notes are statements bearing upon events experienced principally through watching and listening. They contain as little interpretation as possible, and are as reliable as the observer can construct them. Each ON represents an event deemed important enough to include in the fund of recorded experience, as a piece of evidence for some proposition yet unborn or as a property of context or situation. An ON is the Who, What, When, Where, and How of human activity. It tells who said or did what, under stated circumstances.

Each ON is constructed as a unit event that can stand by itself as a datum, or can be fully understood in the context of other ON's on any given date or circumstance. If it records actual conversation, the researcher quotes exact words, phrases, or sentences: otherwise, he uses the apostrophe (single quotes) to indicate somewhat lesser certainty, or he paraphrases as best he can. If the observer wishes to go beyond the "facts" in the instance, he writes a theoretical or inferential note.

TN: Theoretical notes represent self-conscious, controlled attempts to derive meaning from any one or several observation notes. The observer as recorder thinks about what he has experienced, and makes whatever private declaration of meaning he feels will bear conceptual fruit. He interprets, infers, hypothesizes, conjectures; he develops new concepts, links these to older ones, or relates any observation to any other in this presently private effort to create social science.

MN: A methodological note is a statement that reflects an operational act completed or planned: an instruction to oneself, a reminder, a critique of one's own tactics. It notes timing, sequencing, stationing, stage setting, or maneuvering. Methodological notes might be thought of as observational notes on the researcher himself and upon the methodological process itself; as complete a chronicle as the recorder finds necessary or fruitful. Were he to plan on writing for later publication about his research tactics, he would take detailed notes; otherwise his *MN* consists mainly of reminders and instructions to himself.

Putting it all together

When he records, the researcher will tie these three kinds of notes together through a variety of analytic and operational processes. Another example that suggests these processes may suffice here. (The example itself merits some discussion for its own value, as it relates to the oft-voiced question, How many times do you have to record something when it happens frequently?) Let us say that the researcher has observed and recorded an event, that later he discovers he has already recorded a number of events "like" this one. It appears to him that he has created conceptually a *class* of events. Up to this point, his notations have been recorded as discrete ON's. Now, having thought of the event as one of a class, he records the conceptual linkage as a TN. He now has a number of options, depending upon his estimate at the time of the importance of that class for further analysis.

If the class name assigned is a common one and if, for the present, he cannot "make something" of it, he writes in the TN that he had noted this kind of event several times (as ON's), that it is not uncommon, and that he will no longer record such events. He may even "take a stab" at explaining it, relating it perhaps to other classes of event, or "simply" state the conditions under which the event seems to occur. By taking this option he has economized the observing and recording processes, and has momentarily captured a conceptual building block for later analysis. He is now free of the need to note such an event again and again, until such time as it gains new importance by virtue of subsequent observation—as when the discrete events are found to fit better under other classifications.

Were the researcher, however, to judge the class as having some special significance (this judgment can come at any time), he will not only note the class name and other details in the TN but record an MN as well. The MN tells (as reminder or instruction) of an operational decision to look for additional instances and concomitant occurrences to link this event to other events, to persons, or to ideologies. If the researcher has a hypothesis or hunch about the event, he may systematically or casually "test" it. Having performed the task to his immediate satisfaction, he would prepare still another TN on his "findings"—even write a lengthy memo were they to strike him as a major discovery. In the process, the event is conceptually transformed, as is some of his thinking. In this manner, and in many other ways, the recording process serves centrally and critically as a cumulative and developmental aid to the researcher.

Packaging

It is not unusual for a bright person in a new and exciting research situation to find himself so stimulated as to be unwilling or unable to "turn himself off." He may, indeed, be bright enough to draw several inferences from just about every datum noted in the first few days of observation. How the researcher handles his own productivity is a major problem, particularly in the early stages of the research when he cannot seem to get away from the typewriter: he must go to bed with a note pad at his side; everything he hears or reads seems to "trip off" some unrecorded event or nuance now remembered.

As if this problem were not enough, he must also concern himself with later processes, particularly information retrieval; for whatever he may be saying about his experiences now, he knows that later they may be conceptually transformed as new categories emerge in his thinking. Then, he will find it necessary to make "analytic searches" for the older items to bring them to bear upon the emergent ones. How is he later to find them? When the time comes, he will vaguely recall having recorded certain items, but now after weeks of watching, listening and recording he cannot recall exactly where the needed data are. Hence, our model researcher has devised a system for storing and retrieving qualitative information suitable to his own needs—in short, a system of *information control*.

A "package" of data is an abstract rendering, in brief paragraph form (a half dozen sentences or less) which tells of a single, distinct event (ON), draws an inference (TN), or makes a tactical decision (MN). The package is so prepared as later to be scanned and comprehended at a glance. This takes some doing, but once learned, is of inestimable value to any field researcher who must deal mainly with "volumes" of qualitative data. The recorder disciplines himself to think in terms of *units of information,* whatever their content. In the process of making units he learns what a "unit" is, and eventually he develops several models for the different kinds of data he is getting. With some practice, the necessary forethought will take only a few seconds; then the thought is economically rendered. Since the field notes are private documents, no special attention need be paid to grammatical construction, although the item must be clearly intelligible even years later. The package style is helpful, too, to any transcriber who may be asked to type the data from tape for it solves the problem of paragraphing.

When rendering a package, if an additional (even directly related) thought comes to mind the researcher holds it for a time, and then develops another package. Preparation of these packages will often suggest new or additional information, which in turn is packaged as a reminder or suggestion (MN) as to where and when to find it. In his daily recording, the researcher need not concern himself with the specific ordering of items, for this would slow him down too much. Nor is it necessary to invent an interpretation for each field note: the researcher simply packages his observations and ideas as they occur to him.

He avoids excessive concern with the ordering of items for another important reason: he often finds himself reminded of events that he knows he witnessed but had neither noted down nor later recorded—events experienced even many days earlier. He regards these data as no less legitimate than the immediately recorded data. Events "witnessed," but not fully attended to, frequently become knowable when new experiences and thoughts make them meaningful. Then he records them, correctly noting the circumstances or the approximate date of the original experience. He takes the attitude that the inclusion of later-remembered materials has no less significance than do the later redefinitions, dictated by subsequent observations and thoughts, that pertain to the significance of data. After all, the rules that govern what is to be recorded are similar to those that govern watching; since the content of the respective processes are capable of alteration with advancing conception and changes in events, *every experience is recorded when deemed important* and possibly even ignored later.

Page mechanics

In addition to packaging, the scanning process which later is so important to analysis and validation is further facilitated by the frequent use of headings and sub-headings—particularly when the recorder knows in advance that the next several packages will be constructed around some central theme or story line. Also, along an edge of each page he leaves wide margins for the probable addition later of penciled words or phrases that will denote categories or classes of events recorded. Such marginal notes suggest rubrics for later coding; but as penciled, they can easily be changed again and again to reflect new orders of classification as these develop. Nevertheless, they too help with scanning and the location of items.

Also, there is, of course, no more important act in information control than the *dating* of each day's record—even every page. Our researcher securely staples the pages of notes for each date or observational unit. He prepares at least one carbon copy and keeps the copies geographically separate as a precaution against fire, theft or other mishap. Those contingencies, too, are part of the researcher's general field of operations.

Preparing Analytic Memos

Another important property of making field notes is the preparation of *analytic memos*. At times, in the process of developing a TN, the recorder finds that he can elaborate upon the inference, or tie up several inferences in a more abstract statement. Then, rather than cluttering his recording of neat and slim packages with lengthy discussions, he prepares quite a separate analytic memo in which, as much as he cares to, he ramifies his ideas. (For purposes of easy recognition and quick "retrieval," he types these analytic memos on paper which is a different color from the other field notes and files them separately. He will wish to type them himself so they will not languish in the typist's office and so that he can think while he is typing, perhaps elaborating as he continues to type.)

As these analytic memos cumulate, they are likely to become the heart of his final set of ideas, and they lie at the very core of his publication. Whatever his final uses of any given memo, by writing it the researcher is able to develop and put partial closure to some idea. This simultaneously satisfies his need to develop an abstract statement and his need to turn either to other ideas or to concrete operational matters.

In this connection, it is not unusual to find that a single memo will yield an interesting theory or concept, but not one which actually is central to the researcher's immediate purposes at the time of its write-up. That depends upon the degree of his enthusiasm, his pacing of research, and how it relates to his other theoretical memos and their central ideational thrust. (We shall say more about this in the chapter on analysis.) Many a research project itself is part of a longer career, composed of several projects, each of which may be seen as a creative "spin-off" from a larger intellectual endeavor. Whether or not the researcher elects to take the time to develop for immediate publication the idea embodied in his memo, or to include it as part of the later publication based on the current project, he does have a record of the idea.

The Interview File

In addition to preparing field notes and memos, the researcher also finds it necessary to document lengthy conversations and his longer interviews. While reference to them is made in the field notes, a separate but carefully dated file is kept for these items. This file covers a wide range of topics, including the career and general view of that world of each respondent. It may also include one or more sets of formal interviews, covering approximately the same range of topics, with a series of informants. As the number of interviews pile up, it becomes increasingly difficult precisely to remember conversation, context, and perspectives taken by respondents. Interviews of an hour or more may yield a score of typewritten pages.

An excellent device for handling the problem of forgetting, and of later analytic search, is to prepare a single *top sheet*—a summary consisting of a few sentences descriptive of the respondent or of the interview situation, or of any event or idiosyncratic bit of color, all of which may help. Much later the researcher can, for various purposes, leaf through the top sheets asking such questions as whether this or that respondent held a certain perspective. Thus, through this preliminary and rapid scanning, he saves himself hours of work.

Concluding Note

The development of a good set of notes serves many purposes. Besides relieving the researcher of the burdens of remembering events and his thoughts about them and helping him to establish a stable chronicle of experiences and operations, such a set of notes helps in more subtle ways. It becomes the vehicle for ordered creativity. The researcher is restrained by nothing save his sense of honesty and objectivity; since the record is private and no single package is either likely to be published or shown even to colleagues, he is motivated to pour out his observations and thoughts in an intimate, informal manner.

The notes also constitute a written record of the development of the researcher's thoughts about his observations. As he scans his ON's he recognizes the fullness, clarity and incontrovertibility of distinct experiences in the field. These are not "soft data"; these are as hard and true as he could make them from his experiences.

Moreover, the field notes are a stable source of excitement, constantly available for variable and creative constructions. The TN, as a constructive overlay of the ON, represents his struggle with the meaning of his notes. Taken as a kind of datum, the TN as a whole is true of him and a stable record forever; but also it spells development. Any researcher examining his earliest TN's will find a variety of constructs or thoughts about observed events: some foolish enough to bring forth a blush; some brilliantly conceived and subsequently proven in further experience; still others, though quite rational and true, of little value in the context of themes and models subsequently developed.

Nonetheless, he had come to grips with some aspect of human life and had wrestled with it to the point of conceptually transforming his own experience. If his subsequent publication, a "final" rendering of his experiences, brings no acclaim or if it brings him scorn, that is not because of his data—for indeed if he observed, attended to the selection of things observed, and carefully recorded them, then he would have to look elsewhere for what went wrong. In the next chapter we shall examine strategies for analysis that come to grips with the problem of rendering the meaning of one's experience for colleagues and other audiences.

Suggested Reading

No uniform technique for recording qualitative data has emerged to date. Researchers may develop ingenious systems for writing and organizing their data but rarely tell about them, except by way of illustration. Readers might best examine some of the ethnographies listed in the bibliography for Chapter 3, and also refer to the following items, which unfortunately hint at, more than tell, how recording is done.

BOISSEVAIN, JEREMY, "Fieldwork in Malta," in George D. Spindler (ed.), *Being an Anthropologist: Fieldwork in Eleven Cultures,* Chapter 3, pp. 58–84. New York: Holt, Rinehart and Winston, 1970.

Provides some insight into problems of recording data and briefly discusses how he did it.

GEER, BLANCHE, "First Days in the Field," in Phillip Hammond, *Sociologists at Work,* pp. 322–44. New York: Basic Books, Inc., 1964. Also in

McCall-Simmons, *Issues in Participant Observation: A Text and Reader,* pp. 144–62. Reading, Mass.: Addison-Wesley Publishing Co., 1969.

An excellent article dealing with the relations among field notes, final data, inferences, and later analysis of the data.

GLASER, BARNEY, and ANSELM STRAUSS, *Theoretical Sampling.* Forthcoming. Chapter on memo writing.

A system for recording analytical operations after or in tandem with running field notes.

JUNKER, BUFORD H., "Observing, Recording and Reporting," in *Field Work: An Introduction to the Social Sciences,* Chapter 2, pp. 12–31. Chicago: University of Chicago Press, 1960.

Somewhat sketchy but suggestive and useful.

MILLS, C. WRIGHT, *The Sociological Imagination.* New York: Oxford University Press, 1959. See especially pp. 195–226.

Although written basically as a critique of sociology, this book is an impressive account of one social scientist's struggle with the organization (recording and codification) of his intellectual experience.

NORBECK, EDWARD, "Changing Japan: Field Research," in Spindler, *Being an Anthropologist,* Chapter 10, pp. 238–66.

Brief but instructive reference to notes and note taking.

7

Strategy for Analyzing

In virtually every chapter of the book we have made some reference to analysis, but more in terms of how it is linked to other strategies than as a process with its own distinctive properties. Particularly, we have emphasized its simultaneity and continuity with other strategies; also its self-corrective and cumulative character. We require, now, a more pointed discussion of qualitative analysis itself as a set of strategies.

Right off, we need to caution the reader against his own expectations that he may learn from us standard procedures for handling this task of analysis. Qualitative analysts do not often enjoy the operational advantages of their quantitative cousins in being able to predict their own analytic processes; consequently, they cannot refine and order their raw data by operations built initially into the design of the research. Qualitative data are exceedingly complex, and not readily convertible into standard measurable units of objects seen and heard; they vary in level of abstraction, in frequency of occurrence, in relevance to central questions in the research. Also, they vary in the source or ground from which they are experienced. Of course, data also differ according to substance, and, coupled with the ways data are gathered and the forms in which they are apprehended, may lend themselves to different sorts of operations. Little wonder, then, that field researchers cannot predesign their analytic operations with exactness; probably most do not even try.

Not only are the data variable and complex, but so are the analysts. They have had different training and subsequent experiences which, along with their variable temperaments and interests, have produced many analytic styles. Some researchers are satisfied to deal with uncodified, anecdotal data and depend almost entirely upon the fortuitous development of insight; at the other end of the spectrum are those who laboriously codify their data and apply more systematic analytic techniques, including statistical ones, to arrive at social theory.

What Is Analysis?

Our purpose in the present chapter is to help the novice redefine somewhat the concept of analysis—so that he might find it more comfortable to deal with—as *the working of thought processes* rather than as a formidable, academic abstraction. We hope to alter some of the imagery commonly associated with that concept. Our experiences with students lead us to believe that the two most dominant images they associate with the concept of analysis are Science and Insight. Neither is a very comfortable term with which to work. The first bears upon the status of the researcher as "scientist" rather than upon the character of the data and the pragmatic ways that he might work with them. The second bears upon the "genius" of the researcher through which analytic processes take on mystical quality; it offers little room for understanding the craftsmanship involved in the production of theory.

For the novice who is confronted with a mass of heterogeneous data, and who is trying to make sense of them, there is little advantage to be gained from discussing Science and Insight. A discussion of thought processes as strategies is more helpful; for once the components of any craft are understood, then the genius of even its most expert practitioners loses its mystical quality. Their skills may be recognized "simply" as a variation of ordinary thinking and ordinary skills. After all, to be told immediately that $9 \times 9 = 81$ is an act of genius and a mystery, until one comes to know of the existence of the multiplication table. Analytic thinking is not different from ordinary (but yet complex, logical and purposeful) thinking. As with all other aspects of the research process, analyzing data involves thinking that is self-conscious, systematic, organized, and instrumental. It is thinking, objectified and operationalized. Above all, it is extremely active —better still, an interactive process between the researcher and his experience or data—and it is sustained rather than intermittent or casual, as in ordinary thinking.

We need, parenthetically, to develop further a point made earlier bearing upon how one prepares for analyzing and when it may be done. Theoretically or arbitrarily, analyzing can begin when the first data are obtained, or it can begin after much or all of the data are obtained. In one sense, the option may be regarded as a *work strategy,* a matter of convenience in pacing or sequencing one's total work. On the other hand, we have already noted that our model researcher starts analyzing very early in the research process. For him, the option represents an *analytic strategy:* he needs to analyze as he goes along both to adjust his observational strategies, shifting some emphases towards those experiences which bear upon the development of his understanding, and generally, to exercise control over his emerging ideas by virtually simultaneous "checking" or "testing" of these ideas. This is why he prepares TN's as he goes along; for he will not only have a chronicle of his thoughts and some checks bearing upon their usefulness and validity, but will have saved himself from an otherwise crushing task of sorting out a mountain of data without benefit of "preliminary" analysis. Any given TN is—or potentially is—a "mini-proposition" that may even form the core of an analytic scheme; therefore, the systematic development of TN's can be thought of as preliminary analysis.

Discovering Classes and
Their Linkages

Probably the most fundamental operation in the analysis of qualitative data is that of discovering significant *classes* of things, persons and events and the *properties* which characterize them. In this process, which continues throughout the research, the analyst gradually comes to reveal his own "is's" and "because's": he names classes and links one with another, at first with "simple" statements (propositions) that express the *linkages,* and continues this process until his propositions fall into *sets,* in an ever-increasing density of linkages. This, at least, is the operational model the analyst will use when he is attempting to encompass or account for the greater part of his data. Whether his objective is straight description,[1] analytic description,[2] or substantive theory,[3] the task of establishing and linking classes is mandatory.

___

[1] In *straight description,* the analyst accepts and uses theory and organizational schemes that are extant in the discipline: he simply finds classes in the data which correspond with those commonly utilized in the discipline or in more common parlance, and he arranges them accordingly; that is, he links his classes in ways suggested by received classificatory schemes.

[2] In *analytic description,* the organizational scheme is developed from discovered classes and linkages suggested or mandated by the data. Considerable novelty in description is thereby achieved, and with some further development in the analytic process, substantive theory can be made evident.

[3] *Substantive theory* is at least implicit in any description, even in straight de-

Key linkage

The analyst need not, however, link every class to every other, although he will probably have to perform this operation until a guiding metaphor or general scheme emerges in his thinking as he interacts with the data. For once the analyst gains a *Key Linkage*—that is, a metaphor, model, general scheme, overriding pattern, or "story line"—he can become increasingly selective of the classes he needs to deal with: classes to look for, to refine further, or to link up with other classes. The principal operational advantage to the researcher of creating or finding a key linkage is that, for the first time, he has the means of determining the significance of classes. Without it, he must give relatively equal attention to a vast number of the more obvious classes, and consequently will never feel comfortable enough to implement a closure process.

Without the key, one obvious alternative is to gather data until virtually nothing new seems to be coming in. Another alternative is to utilize fully a starting framework and any received theory as a key. Then he will have known all along which classes are significant and, having "located" rather than "discovered" them, he will have concluded his data gathering and most of his analysis rather quickly—and without much sweat (or profit). However, if he is intent upon developing theory, he will have to take the "long route" until he discovers a *grounded* key—one that is both original to him and faithful to his data.

Perhaps at this point we are a bit ahead of ourselves and must return to the model analyst quite early in his research, while he is still working with a starting framework. That framework, or any subsequent experience, may suggest substantive models or organizing schemes, but he makes no commitment to them. Such linkages as he imagines to be suitable will appear implicitly or explicitly in his TN's; these linkages are feelers towards working models suitable to all or portions of the data. (He has yet to enter into a kind of dialogue with his data about their efficacy and validity. Shortly, we shall discuss some of the nature of this dialogue.)

At this time we need to ask, How does the analyst arrive at his classes? We might try to answer this question in part by indicating some sources from which classes (often only as elements in classification systems) come to the attention of the researcher. For practical purposes, we shall identify a few bearing most directly upon social science field research.

---

scription, but there it bears upon received theory. For new, grounded theory to be made evident, the analyst must reveal the metaphor or scheme he has worked with in the analysis. Then, he must transform the metaphor into sociological language, which, though it relates the analyzed object or process to traditional formulations, nevertheless establishes its own identity.

First are the *Common Classes* of the culture generally, which are available to most anyone of a given society to help distinguish between and among the varieties of things, persons, and events. These classes, as names, provide discriminations that lay persons use in their thinking and communication, and that largely define a common or shared reality.

Second are the *Special Classes,* which persons within selected areas of interest or study utilize to distinguish among the things, persons, and events within their own province. We have in mind here two sub-varieties: (1) those inherent in the researcher's collegial group and (2) those inherent in the host group. Thus, the researcher as a social scientist has available to him from his discipline a discriminative array of class categories (in part serving as conceptual framework), which, at least initially, allow him to see and to organize the events at the site—for example, classes of charismatic and bureaucratic leadership, formal and informal structures as classes of organization, and so on.

In contrast to these "collegial classes" are the "host classes," which are also special but which provide, probably, some distinctive differences in discrimination—connotative if not denotative. In medicine are class names for wards, departments, and equipment (things), class names for echelon, specialists, and offices (persons), and class names for procedures, conferences, and work arrangements (events). Many names for special classes are also in common use outside particular areas of discourse, sometimes borrowed from, sometimes introduced into, the common fund of language. However, the ways in which they tie in with still other class terms, particularly as conceptual frameworks, often make them quite different connotatively from the same terms when in common use. The researcher is aware of this, also that special class terms are not necessarily used and understood universally within any specialized area.

Then there are the *Theoretical Classes,* those discovered by the researcher as observer and analyst that are his own constructs, whether their nomenclature is borrowed from other sources or invented. What makes these a very special source is that the classes developed in this process are grounded in the experience of observation in this specific substance, and are demonstrably applicable and useful to its analysis. For example, recall the field notes in Chapter 6 which suggested a class of "professional patients," and a "calculus of patienthood" suggesting a class name for the way any psychiatric hospital may distribute or "dispose" of patients. Since these classes are not available to the researcher until he has observed in the field for some time, he requires the use of common and collegial classes to gain physical and conceptual entrée, and to locate and establish the general boundaries of his field. In time, through observation, newly discovered and conceptualized classes replace the initial ones.

Perhaps we can illustrate with a simple example this process of shifting grounds: In the study of a medical system, the researcher initially expects or is prepared to find evidence of doctors, nurses, hospital, clinic, and so on, and probably he has some model for how these fit together. When he gets to the site and observes for a brief time he finds, indeed, evidence for these classes. However, he learns that this particular hospital is not what he had imagined it to be: it is an "emergency receiving center" and has "contractual arrangements" with other hospitals for long-term treatment. Then, he learns that ideologically and operationally the core of the medical system within which the hospital is embedded is a series of store-front clinics distributed among strategic neighborhoods. Thus, the terms "hospital" and "clinic" are something different from his original expectation and require new conceptualization.

Upon visiting several of the clinics, he finds that each is manned by only one nurse who is assisted by several Licensed Vocational Nurses— a category of nurse with whom he was unfamiliar. Further, he finds, the physicians are not in evidence at the clinics, but are "on call."

We probably need not go any further with this illustration to make the point that the researcher must shift his grounds to accommodate both some changed and new class categories: the hospital is different, there is a new variety of clinic, he has discovered the LVN, and even the physician looks a bit different. Perhaps most important, he has discovered what appears to be an operational philosophy about health delivery that suggests that he should change his original model.

Thus, we can anticipate *the researcher will continue shifting his grounds as he creates or changes his classes, until all his presumed classes are displaced by those based upon observation,* whether his presumptions were essentially correct or not. He will then have a set or sets of theoretical classes, tested in experience and amenable to linking and to theory construction.

An Illustration of an Analysis

Certainly, it is not enough simply to discover classes, although this is a difficult task in itself, since it requires that their properties and boundaries also be ascertained before propositions bearing upon how they link to each other can be hypothesized and validated. What we require now is a more complicated and detailed illustration of how the linking process might be handled, and how the analyst arrives at his key linkages. The example we use here is a reconstruction of processes engaged in by the authors in a research venture a few years back. Since we must be brief, to indicate the many classes with which we were working, we refer the reader to *Psychiatric Ideologies and Institutions* (see bibliography). Here, we shall attempt to reconstruct some of the processes leading to the discovery of the conceptual scheme around which the book was organized.

Our illustration involves the study of a relatively small (80 bed), private psychiatric hospital consisting of five wards; also a relatively large complement of attending physicians, residents, nurses and nurses' aides.

The field researchers consisted of a team of three persons, the two present authors and one other colleague. We worked much in the manner outlined in the chapters on watching and listening. We divided our labor, prepared and shared our respective field notes, and frequently met to tell each other of our experiences. We had had practically no direct experience with psychiatry—and very little with medicine generally—prior to undertaking the research. With the very barest of frameworks, organized essentially around a general understanding that there were several different treatment philosophies at the hospital, we set about to discover how the many professionals there managed to organize and carry out their respective and collective tasks. Naturally, as social scientists, we were prepared to find that this social order was governed mainly by rules and norms. Yet, we held this hypothesis most tentatively to maximize the possibility of discovering a social order developed along different lines.

True to our own research philosophy, we hesitated making early commitments to conceptualization about the structure of relations among the hospital staff; consequently, our early field notes were exceedingly rich in detailed vignettes of encounters between and among the staff of the several echelons working there. In a sense, each vignette was a discrete story; and sometimes several vignettes constituted a longer story. Their early examination revealed among whom these encounters occurred—just about everyone there, within and between all echelons—among attending men, between attending men and residents, residents and nurses, nurses with attending men, and so on. Indeed, we discovered frequent encounters among all the logical possibilities for encounter. Not so incidentally, we were thereby able to discover the classes and sub-classes of personnel at the site. Then, an examination of the observational notes revealed that many, if not most, of the encounters occurred "incidentally," that is, at the point —and around the time—of some new or problematic incident or happening. Since we had observed that the staff encountered each other at still other occasions, such as at scheduled meetings, we were able to establish an "incidental" class of encounter.

Encounter content: rules versus informal agreements

What were these encounters all about? By simply scanning the vignettes we were able to classify varieties of content: transfers of patients from one ward to another; controls over patients through the use of drugs (including discussions or arguments over whether drugs should be used for this purpose); the "privileges" that patients might be granted (to use the phone, leave the ward unescorted); and who among the staff was to do what, and how, with the patients. There were many other substantive types of encounter besides these. Especially noteworthy and interesting were those involving special arrangements or agreements among personnel; for example, the head nurse balking at the assignment to her ward of a patient deemed "inappropriate" to that ward, and the physician asking her to "take him just for a few days, until. . . ." Among other things, an incident such as this allowed us to create such classes as "patient fit" and "misfit"; "overt" and "covert" agreements; also special classes of agreements, whereby certain nurses and physicians—or any jurisdictional combination —had long histories of such arrangements with consequences for who would side with whom when even more crucial issues arose.

As sociologists—and even as laymen—we were often surprised to find so many private agreements, so many expectantly (by us) ruled procedures become the subject of so many encounters. We began to ask the staff about the rules and norms governing the institution. To our surprise, we found very few able to list more than one or two beyond those governing fire and flood. We knew there were formal agreements among the staff because these were established at scheduled meetings that we also attended; yet, we also saw private agreements, which would bend or break the more formal ones, being made constantly. At about this time we, the researchers, began to use such terms as "pacting," "forming alliances," and "special agreements." Also, we noted that the alliances or pacts bearing upon virtually any agreement were often very short-lived, since any professional, at most any time, could make a new agreement or alliance with someone which frequently forced a revision or breakage in some previous agreement made with someone else. The frequent cries of "betrayal" added evidence for the many broken compacts.

It seemed that we were "on to something," but we still weren't certain of what this was; so we continued to pursue the general phenomena of "pacting" and "agreement-making." Continued examination of the data helped raise additional questions bearing upon why the staff seemed to find it so difficult to reach agreement on what seemed to us such ordinary problems as patient privileges, transfers, and general control of patients.

Our starting framework gave one clue to this question, namely, *differential treatment ideology*. We had originally planned to administer a detailed questionnaire to all the staff bearing on treatment philosophies. This was done, and in addition the fieldworkers interviewed staff on their philosophies while also observing them at work. As expected, we found some major differences among them, and we were able to attribute many of the pacts, agreements, broken agreements and misunderstandings to differential treatment ideologies.

But the staff did not exactly argue ideology in an abstract sense; they argued operations bearing upon real patients in real situations. It was then that we discovered another concept that seemed to explain why even ideologues do not always carry on their work according to ideological dictates. These professionals developed *operational philosophies* as a median ground between pure idea and the pragmatic necessities of collaborating with others of different ideological faith.

Indeed, their work had to do with treating and caring for patients, although it often seemed to us that the staff was far more concerned with each other than with the patients. What was now most important to us was that we could begin to explain *why* this concern with each other was so important to the staff. The work that these professionals had to do by way of treatment and care had to be operationally manifest through agreements bearing upon such mundane but necessary matters as the ward placement and transfer of patients and patient control. To do all of this in the absence of hard-and-fast rules and norms—which could hardly be implemented, much less written down—the staff had to reach agreements, day-to-day, on large numbers of very concrete issues bearing on the handling and disposition of patients.

Meanwhile, we were raising questions about where these treatment ideologies had come from. Quite empirically, we related the various ideologies to the *professional careers* of the professionals and to the *career models* which they were developing and living out. Data for these concepts and relationships came in copious amounts from our interviews with most of the staff. Widely different backgrounds in training and other experiences in psychiatry were evident.

By this time we had assembled many propositions about careers, and an equally cogent set of propositions about treatment ideologies. We had long since done the same for institutional structure through observations of the intricately complex operations of staff on the five wards. It did not, then, require a giant step for us to reach our concept *arena* which helped us link —locatively and situationally—our developed sets of propositions on professions and careers, ideologies, and institutions. Now we were able to view each ward as a location and arena where varying professionals could be found at different stages in their respective careers, adhering to varying ideologies, and implementing ideologies and career models through their development of operational philosophies that were compatible with institutional structures and requirements.

From this vantage point, we were able to reach our prime linkage—

negotiated order—which allowed us to "cross-cut" every one of the sub-sidiary conceptual links, and relate to each our major classes. Our analysis, then, was essentially complete: We were confident that our major and minor classes, concepts and linkages had a maximum of explanatory power. Also, we believed we had discovered a theory—a class of social institutional order—grounded in primary, empirical data.

A final point on the above description of our analysis: given the limitations of writing as a form of communication, and the practically insurmountable task of showing *exactly* how we applied complex and varied analytic procedures to highly complex data, we can only hope that the reader now, very generally, understands how we worked in that particular research situation. By no means have we attempted a full description. We do not wish to leave the reader with the impression that our analysis of our data was the only one or the only legitimate one.

But that in general is how we proceeded, moving back and forth between gathering and analyzing the data. The two processes sometimes are virtually simultaneous, although more often they are separate in time: sometimes separate by some days or weeks, sometimes occuring during the course of the same day or even hours. At any event, the analytic processes are "grounded" in the data—where "grounded" means *both* interpretation of the data and checking upon that interpretation by the gathering of more data.

Conceptual Levering

In preparing this chapter, we had in mind two beginning researchers—one who had done most of his data gathering with care given to its organization and ideation, and one whose data are not only poorly organized but exciting to him only in an intuitive sense. The former novice is well along with his analysis, having prepared TN's and Memos that give him some analytic advantage over his experiences; he is probably headed towards the kind of structural analysis just depicted.

The latter novice poses a more serious problem, mainly because he had no clear analytic goal or research model when he began to gather his data. Perhaps he expected that his data and his "genius" would eventually determine the outcome of his study: ethnographic description, substantive theory, formal theory, or "merely" a few cogent concepts that might shed some light on some especially interesting processes he had observed. Now, surrounded by data, he is probably at the mercy of whatever form and content they present to him. What is he to do? He may not understand or appreciate the kind of structural analysis we have proposed; he may feel his data warrant another kind of treatment.

It may help now to discuss a number of techniques the analyst might use to gain conceptual leverage on his data, either as a preanalytic strategy or as analysis itself, depending upon the state that the data are in. By "lever" we mean any thinking device that both distances the analyst from his data and provides a new perspective on them, so that he may enter into a new relationship with his data. A major problem is that the data do not "speak for themselves"; they barely hint at something, and then only if someone is able to hear. "Hearing" in this sense is an active pursuit of meaning, but only if the listener has some conceptual apparatus to begin with. Unfortunately, data do not leap off the pages to provide the analyst with the insight or genius he needs to "carry it off." This suggests the need for an active discussion, in the context of a triad, among the analyst, an audience, and the data. There are two general possibilities: one where the analyst attempts to gain leverage over his data by communicating them to an audience; the other where the analyst more directly interrogates his data in preparation for later communication.

Communicating the Data

Assuming that the data are more scattered than organized, that the form they are in does not tell a straight nor consistent "story" nor offer a thematic representation of the research experience, then probably the best first step is to develop an elemental description of what was observed. By "elemental" we mean a straightforward, detailed "laying-out" of the significant classes and their properties of the scenes observed: the people there, their understandings, and their activities. Many practiced ethnographers do as much, and make contributions to knowledge in precisely this way.

Lest the researcher get bogged down trying to write for a conjured audience of social science sophisticates, he might try first conjuring a more mundane audience, to pry loose a "good story." "Audience conjuring" often proves effective as a levering process. Since one can hardly write or say anything without there being some real or imagined audience to receive it, any description necessarily will vary according to the audience to which it is directed. Audiences "tell" what substances to include, what to emphasize, and the level and complexity of abstractions needed to convey essential facts and ideas. Since the researcher is party to this dialogue (and audience to himself), he will probably get to know his data better—that is, get to know the data in new ways and thereby discover new properties and linkages in them.

The logic of this procedure, given this stage of data development, is to make it necessary for the analyst to invent an organizational scheme for his data. For in the process of organizing a description, the analyst will be unable to escape having to provide some of the more cogent categories he will need: classes and names for them; relationships among these classes, and names for them too. Moreover, he will not be able to do all this without also providing connective categories necessary to even the most ordinary communication: locative (in time and space), sequential, causal, correlative, consequential. How can anyone describe a complex, ongoing scene without coming to terms with process, or describe social relations— other than in list form—without developing a sense or model of structure?

Moreover, the analyst will necessarily be forced to create priorities for his experience, selectively ignoring some—he cannot include every one— relegating some to the status of context or background, and placing others into the foreground of his description. In this process, he will at least have implicitly established a number of propositional statements and, if the least bit inventive, he will have coined terms or phrases which may constitute key concepts for any later analysis he may wish to pursue.

In addition to audience conjuring (for purposes of writing description), the researcher might also try telling his story to a live audience, especially an interested and sympathetic colleague. There is, we think, a qualitative difference between writing and telling; for many of our readers this may be painfully true as they "tell it beautifully" and then block at writing the same representation. Likewise, there is a qualitative difference between talking to a person and to a tape recorder. We suggest, then, that some researchers might seek out live audiences, and make telling the story a lever. Live interaction exhibits important properties, and more than ordinary "feedback" is implied here. When one speaks to another about something, one also speaks to oneself; hence, the speaker may be a greater stimulant to himself than is the (other) listener.

What are the possibilities here? The listener's comments may "catalyze" the data for the speaker; the listener's questions may "catalyze" the speaker; the speaker may "catalyze" the data in the process of telling it without much overt help from the listener. If any of these consequences of communication occur, the researcher will have levered himself into a new relationship to his own data.

Interrogating the Data

Whether or not the analyst achieves leverage on the data by communicating them to others, and if so, whatever the outcome, he must finally consult his data directly. He must put to the test whatever ideas he may have developed about what the data have to say. If, until then, he has developed no exciting ideas, he must tease them out of the data, and when he gets them feed them back for a test—that is, search for supporting and negative evidence. The analyst cannot *tell* the data what to say. However, he may question them, or pose as queries the cogency and the validity of models, general concepts and metaphors. In reply the data might answer "yes," "no," "maybe"—the latter reply signalling there is too little supporting evidence for the idea, or possibly that the idea, though supportable, is not particularly cogent.

What to ask of data

But how does the analyst know what to ask the data: what models to pose, and operations to perform? We suggest he make use of two mutually supporting sets of levers—one substantive, one logical—for gaining the distance and the variability in perspective that will provide the questions and the models. The *substantive* set is made up of the special, abstract vocabulary of the analyst's own discipline—in the social science, such concepts as institution, ideology, work, career, collective behavior, social movement, and charisma. These concepts are often clustered and provide frameworks that will help the analyst *start* his questioning. We say "start" only to alert the novice to the dangers of using these received concepts *finally* to define and to organize the reality with which he has been dealing. They are, however, perfectly good and useful levers for preliminary analysis; they provide perspective. Consider the concepts "institution" and "social movement": Although they both deal with the affairs of people working in concert, they nevertheless evoke very different kinds of imagery and ideation. In short, to apply either to the data gives one a different perspective or angle of "vision" from the other.

The second set of levers is primarily the *logical, operational armamentarium of science,* for example, experimental, comparative, historical, analogical thinking and working processes. All of these—and still other processes, such as setting up polarities—provide considerable differences in perspective as well as of operation and so help produce the ideas that link datum to datum in various configurations. Most analysts develop skills and styles around these operations, and probably select problems and data that "lend themselves" to favored analytic operations: some analysts use the comparative method and are virtually ahistorical; others think experimentally and some even confine their research to this form; still others work most effectively through analogy and metaphor. However, these are not mutually exclusive forms of operation, and certainly not of speculation and thought.

Ordinarily, any analyst will utilize at least one component in each array as a set of levers for analyzing his data. Unless he has made a commitment to a particular analytic combination sometime before, or early in the research, the analyst will think about and test various combinations once he has most of his data before him. If his data are substantively rich and varied, he may find that certain operations will work better for some portions of the data than others.

To illustrate the utility of a substantive-logical lever combination: imagine observing a city substantively through the eyes (perspective) of a lay homeowner, a realtor, an urban planner, and an urban historian; then vary the position of observation, logically, by walking along the streets, by bicycling and motoring through it and then flying just above it in a helicopter. Assuming one were able to take these perspectives, in combination, the city as "data" would naturally present itself in a variety of conceptual patterns.

Working with abstract forms

Novices occasionally, if not characteristically, bog down in their attempts to utilize substantive levers because they view them as real forms. Experienced researchers and scholars more often see through these abstract devices to the ordinary, empirical realities they represent; they are thereby capable of considerable conceptual mobility. Thus, we urge the novice in analysis to convert relatively inert abstractions into stories—even with plots—in order to induce themes and models that link datum to datum.

Better still, he might best go directly to the data to *discover* "institution" or "social movement"; they evoke different kinds of stories. This way, the analyst escapes the formal stereotype inherent in the concepts; he deals with very human and live phenomena that are amenable to story-making and probably productive of new constructs. The story line can always, later, be reconverted to formal terminology, should the analyst find it necessary. In the meantime, he deals comfortably and naturally with what appears only as description and illustration, but which is but a short distance, conceptually, from generalized social process.

Combining levers

A similar process can be applied to the logical levers as well, although here the questions take different form. Rather than deal separately with substantive and logical questions, let us illustrate their combined uses—again, bearing in mind that we are dealing with starting levers that stimulate thinking. Any valid idea, worth a few minutes of thought, should be carried forward to the limits of its conceptual usefulness; it may become a central or sub-theme, or simply function catalytically for still another idea.

Imagine now that the researcher has his data before him and is in a quandary on how to proceed. Since the data are already gathered, and unless he can return to the site for an extended period, he cannot work the experimental lever. Practically, the options left to him are *comparative* and *historical* levers.

Let us suppose the researcher has some very rich data on a service institution. The institution is organized into several segments—wards, services, or offices, all of which are organizationally and structurally similar and therefore suggestive of comparative analysis. He decides to use the comparative lever; the data allow him to do so. Then he searches for substantive handles and comes up with *leadership, communications,* and *division of labor.* He works with these for a time, and finds it rather discouraging that, though his data offer many suggestions, they are too thin for direct development.

Then, are these data really that "rich" after all? The analyst may raise the question on what substances the data *do* offer him analytic possibilities; and he may, for a time, suffer through having to construct new substantive rubrics to find out what he does have. In this process, he discovers that, at the time he was observing, there was much going on at the institution having to do with some personnel leaving the institution and new ones being hired. He thereby finds himself a *substantive* lever—something to do with "succession." That he has this data in considerable abundance is a function in part of his having exercised relatively little control over his observations; but it is also due to an historical (temporal) condition of the institution at the time he was there, whatever his original intention may have been. He then begins to see (perspective) that the succession of personnel at the institution provides him with a lever on much of his other data: succession activity highlights many structural and organization properties of the several services that he now knows in new ways. As a matter of fact, by virtue of perspective it now becomes clear how these other data can be used—they can be built around his central substance.

Now the questions that he poses to the data can give the affirmative answers he needs, since the data are rich enough for development along the above lines. What about "succession"; how would he define it? Perhaps he has some difficulty here, and decides he can wait until he is more familiar with his data on succession. Looking at the data from this perspective he finds that succession occurred on three of the services, and in two of them not at all; further, that where it occurred, it involved three distinct echelons of personnel. There is, he now sees, an obvious opportunity to compare succession with nonsuccession, and succession in one echelon with two others.

Then it may occur to him that he has two general problems: the first one having to do with the *process* of unseating and seating personnel, and the second with the differential *consequences* of these processes—per service, per echelon—for leadership, communication, and division of labor as these reflect off the succession process.

Indeed, now that he has looked over his data from this perspective, he finds that what he has on leadership, and the other two "aborted" levers deals mainly with the succession problem in the institution studied. Now the analyst is relatively secure, both in his understanding of the data and how he must now proceed. He can now begin to ask about, and search for answers to, differential mechanisms (per service, per echelon) for unseating one person and for seating his replacement. If some had quit with "regret" and with due notice, and others were fired and left in haste, then the analyst has still other comparative possibilities.

Of course, it may occur to him that he does not have a sufficient number of cases to do a "proper" comparative analysis along several variable lines. Yet, this is the data he has; it is at least suggestive if not definitive of any generalizations he may develop around the problem of succession. He can think of his generalizations as hypothetical and promise himself to do another related study in another similar institution, or farther afield in institutions that are organized differently and do different kinds of work. In that event, he would be reaching out from *substantive* theory bearing upon a given institution or type of service to more *formal theory of a social process* applicable to many kinds of institutions and associations.

But to return to the question that the analyst may pose: What do the data tell about mechanisms for replacement? About how loyalties to the displaced persons are handled? About processes of disengagement on the part of those leaving and those being left behind? About the interim period? Then, there are questions about the selection of replacements: who is involved, what sorts of negotiation go on and expectations developed by negotiators; also, differentially depending upon the level of the replacement, how are the new people ushered in, how are they socialized, and who does the coaching? Also what sorts of claims are made by the new people? How are these expressed and dealt with by the old-timers? Finally, what happens to old agreements and rules that bound those who left and now confront the successors with their different identities?

Throughout this entire interrogation, the novice can call upon his extensive experience, wherever it may have been—to conjure a story line of how this process gets worked out anywhere, for *past experience is also a lever.* The analyst will not, of course, inject into his data something experienced earlier or elsewhere, but he would be foolish not to look for events that are suggested by experiences. For example, he may at one time have been party to a "messy situation," wherein a colleague of his was fired from a job, and he remembers many consequences of that event. From that experience he may even be able to work out a model of "cooling out" the displaced person and of his allies who were left behind, and then search his own data for parallels and differences. This may lead him to a subsidiary perspective on his data bearing upon the tactics and countertactics of firing and hiring, of alliances, of processes of exacting concessions in exchange for "keeping the peace."

As to the analyst's other discovered problem (the differential consequences to the various services and to the entire institution of the succession process), he has still other questions to ask: What changes occurred in the division of labor, differentially, in the various services? How about differential impact depending upon the echelon which had the replacement? The analyst traces or tracks down consequences of the events for leadership and for communication; but he may also, by this time, have discovered new classes he did not know existed before as some persons at the site "lined up" pro and con in new combinations.

He may also have discovered that the consequences of succession for the clients being served by the institution were not considerable. But he may have too little data on this aspect of the research to make valid propositions. In that event, he must suffer the consequences of his own failure—while in the field—to have asked the kinds of questions he is now belatedly posing. He may now understand why he can evaluate his data as good or bad, for they are either only to the extent they help him answer his present questions.

Our model researcher—the first novice—had been raising these questions all along during his research, and had been guided by them to build density into his ON's and TN's. He had developed a language and a grounded framework: claims, negotiations, tactics, consequences, and the like—some newly coined, some borrowed from other special languages. With cogent as well as copious data, he is better able than his counterpart (to whom we have been addressing ourselves) to find answers to his questions. However, each novice in his own way had come to realize that in working particular data he had discovered both *general processes* and *general questions* applicable to other fields.

Another lesson learned is that not every bit of data need be included in the final scheme; that is, except for negative evidence that may invalidate the final statement, the researcher need not pursue his original intention to prepare a description of his whole experience. Researchers frequently "spin off" pieces of a whole for publication and later, if not satiated, go on to other segments of the field. The "whole," after all, is a construct; and the "part" dealt with may later be redefined as the whole. This is but another illustration of how new perspective and discovery may alter "reality."

Historical questions

Let us now shift our attention to historical questions to show how ideas may be generated and analysis sparked. We shall use a social movement as our illustration. As with the data on the service institution, there is an apparent richness, but again the analyst cannot gain sufficient or significant leverage. He has spent several months somewhat systematically visiting among locales identifiable (in common parlance) as "hippie-type" communes. Common and special vocabularies describe members of this movement as having become "alienated," "turned off," "anti-establishment," and now in their new life as "tuned in" and "doing their own thing." Most of the data tell about relationships among members living in these communes; lesser amounts tell of the work they do there, of their ceremonies and rituals; and many interviews offer data on the beliefs these people hold about themselves and about the "established" society they despise.

Of course, the analyst may do some comparative analysis, since he had been to many communes that exhibit strikingly similar as well as dissimilar attributes. He also has data, based primarily upon interviews, which tell how persons in the movement became involved in it. In examining these data, the analyst is drawn to two kinds of historical levers: the first is based upon the longitudinal and career models embedded in the empirical data that he has; the second lever is more social-philosophical, bearing upon the model of social forms emerging out of general social-cultural properties characteristic of a time or era in the life of a society. On the latter, the analyst has no ready data nor ideas grounded in his current research experience. Yet he may raise questions prompted by this model to help him see the theoretical possibilities in the data which he does have.

Historical versus comparative analysis

A word first about the relationship between historical and comparative analysis; they are not in all respects distinctive. If our analyst were to compare a social form with itself at an earlier stage in its own history, he would be simultaneously thinking historically and comparatively. He would also be doing so if he were to examine his own movement against a backdrop of readings on the "Bohemian" and "Beat" movements of some decades past. Imagine a chess board with the horizontal squares providing comparative social forms, and the vertical squares offering temporal stages in their development. If our analyst were to "place" his movement in a center square, and then imagine expressive movements in the squares to the left and political reform movements to the right of it, he would then have prepared a *comparative base* across the theoretical board of social movements. He would also have a basis for comparing historically the various stages of development of each movement. Even if he were to have no primary data on the other movements, some readings on them would probably spark many questions bearing directly upon his own data. For example, from what strata of the general population did these movements spring? (social class, age, sex, region and so on). What were these people doing occupationally prior to joining the movement? To what extent did joining the movement constitute a total commitment? What sorts of social organization evolved among members of each? What kinds of rituals, ceremonies and norms of interpersonal conduct developed and at what stages?

If the analyst were to do this kind of semisystematic reading and questioning, he would have attained both comparative and historical perspective, and the distance necessary for a new look at his own direct experience. Where was this movement some two or three years ago in organization, membership, beliefs? Are the same kinds of people still being recruited into it now? How did the relations between the sexes evolve? It is our guess that in this process of questioning, the analyst will have discovered distinctions not only between his own movement and others but also within the various segments of his own. Thus, he might further subdivide the square within which he was working and sort out several sub-typical segments. Once again he can apply the same kinds of questions to each of these.

The comparability of data

An important implication of what we just wrote is that, in the social sciences, one never really studies even a single case of some social phenomenon without at least implicitly making internal distinctions that are amenable to comparison. Also, it is difficult to imagine the study of a case without suggesting how it relates to *other* realities of like and different kind on the same plane. Otherwise, would our analysis be social science? How, also, would anyone read the case without temporal-spatial reference and without social-cultural context that might suggest *general conditions* of which this case is a single instance.

We need make a distinction between the operations of our two novices bearing upon the ideas just presented. In the case of the second novice, who is not likely to return to the field, the reading and the thinking about comparison groups functions primarily as a *stimulant* to operations on the data he has. For our model researcher, the operational possibilities are greater, since he can build the product of his comparative thinking directly into his own data as they are discovered, as well as have it help with observation in the field.

Some contemporary methodologists insist that the only valid data are those which the researcher himself gathers. We think not. *Concepts, models, and even data drawn from examinations of secondary sources can be utilized directly and openly by the researcher in any way which facilitates his understanding, not only of his field, but of any other field that conceptually bears upon discovered generalizable processes.*

Suggested Reading

BARTON, ALLEN H., and PAUL F. LAZARSFELD, "Some Functions of Qualitative Analysis in Social Research," *Frankfurter Beitrage zu Sociologie,* I (1955), 321–61. Also in McCall-Simmons, *Issues in Participant Observation: A Text and Reader,* pp. 163–96. Reading, Mass.: Addison-Wesley Publishing Co., 1969.

A lengthy article suggesting useful modes of analyzing qualitative data; some excellent suggestions (models) for levering data.

BECKER, HOWARD S., "Problems of Inference and Proof in Participant Observation," *American Sociological Review,* XXIII (1958), 652–60. Also in McCall-Simmons, *Issues in Participant Observation,* pp. 245–54.

A systematic discussion of basic analytic processes carried on in field work; consideration given to such important matters as the credibility of qualitative data and their frequency and distribution.

BECKER, HOWARD S., and BLANCHE GEER, "Participant Observation: Analysis of Qualitative Data," in R. N. Adams and J. J. Preiss (eds.), *Human Organization Research,* pp. 267–89. Homewood, Ill.: The Dorsey Press, 1960.

Excellent article supporting the logic of field work through a discussion of the organization and analysis of qualitative data.

GLASER, B., and ANSELM STRAUSS, *Discovery of Grounded Theory: Strategies for Qualitative Research.* Chicago: Aldine Publishing Co., 1967.

An influential work offering a distinct perspective on the analytic uses of qualitative data for the discovery and understanding of social processes. See especially Chapter 5, "The Constant Comparative Method of Qualitative Analysis," which may also be found in *Social Problems,* XII (1965), 436–45.

STRAUSS, ANSELM, et al., *Psychiatric Ideologies and Institutions.* New York: The Free Press, 1964. See especially Chapter 2, pp. 18–22.

A small list of items on organizing and analyzing qualitative data which complements our current discussion.

8

Strategies for Communicating
the Research

We had originally planned to develop separate chapters for validating the research findings and for telling and writing about them. However, since research is ultimately addressed to audiences that selectively and variously judge its validity, these apparently disparate processes can logically be combined into a single discussion. One may argue that the researcher ought best to address himself to the canons of Science rather than to audiences, which, in contrast, are more ephemeral and often ideological. Yet, even the canons of Science are the product of human thinking, of human groups that define and sustain them. Besides, the researcher must very practically address himself to people, even if also to Science.

Then which people or groups does he tell of his work? Should he select only those who represent themselves as methodologically expert? What a pity, and a bore! Even among methodologists within the social sciences there are sharp differences in perspective on what is, and what is not, acceptable research. But perhaps this is a philosophical or ideological issue we had best not deal with here. We prefer simply to take a sociological, and practical, position on the question, and write mainly about the researcher communicating with audiences he is likely to encounter in the course of and as a consequence of his research. Questions about the validity and reliability of the research can then be examined in the context of communications with those who would judge it.

We are aware that many of our readers are graduate students with pressing problems in writing up their research, bearing particularly upon methodological issues; therefore, we shall not neglect to discuss strategies for handling this problem. These students face faculty committees, which can be most exacting and critical. Because there are so few faculty on a committee, and because they play such a special role in that capacity, they tend to represent relatively narrow substantive and methodological interests. Yet they are so powerful! Little wonder, then, that so many students do their research exclusively for this audience and ignore any others.

It may be of some comfort for students to know that even accomplished researchers do not also escape close scrutiny and judgment: "readers" who help publishers decide whether to publish articles or books can be harsh indeed; and after books are published, writers can await very harsh critiques published as "reviews" in many different journals. However, it is not unusual to find both praising and damning reviews appear simultaneously in separate journals, attesting both to the politics of criticism and to the variability in criteria used in passing judgment. Yet, we suppose the established researcher still has considerable advantage over the student, since his reputation will probably help him find a publisher willing enough to give the writer access to multiple audiences with wide and compatible interests.

Multiple Audiences and
Communication

During any stage of his study, the researcher is likely to be in communication with one or another audience about the substance or methods of his research. These audiences will vary widely in how they relate to the research as a project, to the research findings and operations, and even to the researcher as a person: They comprehend, selectively use, and judge the work from a variety of perspectives and interests. Some audiences are methodologically sophisticated and take an interest in the research almost solely in terms of the acceptability (to them) of the research procedures used; other audiences are interested primarily in gleaning substantive ideas, and validate or invalidate them informally according to their own experiences, intuitions, and logic. But this example—presented as a polarity—indicates only one dimension in the variability of audiences and their respective modes and criteria of judgment.

Before discussing particular audiences and ways of dealing with them, we shall tell in advance of two central points we wish to make in this concluding chapter. The first takes us back to what we had written earlier in the book about the nature of *reality:* that it is neither fixed nor finite, that it is infinitely complex, and that the observer holds the key to an infinitely varied relationship with "it." Well, audiences are observers too, and they, no less than the researcher, hold keys to understanding it. Therein lies the essence of a central problem in communication as it affects the researcher: he must make judgments on specific and general interests his audiences may have, on what sorts of information they might appreciate, need, or demand, and what their sense of credibility will allow them to accept.

This leads us to the second point: the researcher—just as he must decide on what to look at, listen for, and analyze—must likewise make decisions on whom to tell, what and how much to tell, and how and when to tell. Similarly for writing: when to write (during or after the research), for what audience(s), and how. Such decisions rest upon assumptions of the researcher on what his audiences will accept as important and valid; therefore, he needs to anticipate the kinds of questions that his varying audiences will pose and decide how he will later defend his data, his ideas, and his methods.

Now we have come "full circle" back to our proposition that the researcher will meet many audiences with varying expectations on substance, and with varying standards for establishing the credibility of what they read or hear. Of course, the number and range of audience types will differ for each researcher; his options to avoid, lightly entertain, or seriously meet "head on" these different audiences will vary, as will the risks entailed for avoiding or making contact. Also, the researcher will experience variable conditions for engaging with audiences in informal conversation, "informal" seminars, formal speeches and different orders of formal writing. If the reader were to take into account and "cross cut" the variables written into this paragraph, he would be well along towards developing a structural model for communication during and after a given species of research project.

Let us consider now what might be a typical course of audience encounters experienced by our model researcher. If he is a student, most of his work will have been preceded by a series of conferences with one or more professors; if he is a postdoctoral fellow or young professional, he will have played the joyous game of "grantsmanship" with a funding agency, and probably will have consulted with colleagues and "old pro's" at the game to help bolster his case with the granting committee of the agency. Already, he will have encountered several audiences to whom he has stated his problem and fashioned his research plan. Now at this stage, and with these audiences particularly, he has convinced very powerful others of his own abilities to fulfill the overall requirements of the research, to understand the relationship between what he is about to do and what his forebears have already done in that area, and to finish the task. All of this probably with little or no data.

Host audiences

In addition to the aforementioned classes of audience, the researcher will have confronted varieties of hosts in the field setting. This set of encounters has already been dealt with at some length in an earlier chapter. It should be borne in mind that the hosts have their own particular identities (real or self-styled) as administrators, policy-makers, practitioners, "activists," theorists, and even researchers. These same identities are also found outside the research field: leaders of other, but similar, organizations and movements may be no less interested in the substance of the research findings, in solutions to very practical problems affecting themselves, and in the implications of the research for broader policy development and organizational work. Thus, once the researcher is well along, or finished with his data gathering and preliminary analysis, he can begin to map out some of the available options concerning whom to write to, whom to speak to, and what to say.

Even if he were doing the research as a thesis necessarily addressed in part to his faculty committee, he will still have many other audiences with whom to communicate: his closest colleagues, his own more general colleagueship or profession, the larger group of which his hosts in the field are only a segment, varieties of lay audiences with real and sustained interests in the field he has researched, and so on.

Levels of Publication

Social psychologically, it is the multiplicity of audiences and the researcher's awareness of others' perspectives and information needs that account for much of the complexity in the researcher's thinking; in turn this accounts for the complexity of the data which he will or has gathered. Therefore, the researcher may simultaneously prepare several presentations directed at many audiences: a written piece for the "house organ" of the hosts, one for a popular magazine answering to a general public interested in social commentary, and another for one of the researcher's own professional journals. There are many other possibilities: a talk or an article on his methods of field research, on the development of his theory, on the implications of his findings for policy-making, and several different presentations bearing upon different topical aspects of his research.

For each of these presentations, the proffered data, and the researcher experience generally, are shaped to an audience; the form of the presentation is also audience directed: general essays, polemical articles, social commentaries, scientific tracts, descriptive monographs. The language used and the topics emphasized will differ according to the audience in order to effect not only good, but comfortable and mutually interesting communications. This way, the data can be "mined" for several years in a multitude of ways and for many audiences—and many a researcher has done just that.

In preparing for any telling or writing, and in imagining the perspective of his specific audience, the researcher is apt to see his data in new ways: finding new analytic possibilities, or implications he has never before sensed. This process of late discovery is full of surprises, sometimes even major ones, which lead to serious reflection on what one has "really" discovered. Thus, it is not simply a matter of the researcher writing down what is in his notes or head; writing or telling as activities exhibit their own properties which provide conditions for discovery. Once the products of these unintended consequences are apprehended, they are generally incorporated into still later speeches and writings, and in the "final" writing.

Likewise, once the researcher has told or written his account—whatever its content and form, and for whatever audience—thoughtful criticism and questions from any audience will suggest further reflection, and possibly some revisions in thinking about the data or about the ideas generated in preparation for the communication. As a communicator the researcher takes criticism in stride, and selectively deals with it. Some criticism goes directly to any weakness the research may have had; some is "misplaced," possibly because of failure in the communication itself, or because the content or style of the communication was directed at the "wrong" audience. Any journal or magazine, for example, will "turn down" a submitted article which does not meet its requirements for form or content; it, too, has audiences. But this does not necessarily reflect upon the validity or usefulness (to still others) of the communication. If the research itself is an honest work and the findings grounded and original, the persistent researcher will surely find or create his audience. Quite possibly, the researcher will speak with or write for an audience just to "try out" his ideas, and simultaneously to get some feedback.

Establishing Credibility

For graduate students and impecunious researchers, shopping for audiences is no easy matter; faculty committees and research-grant review committees are like company stores to which most shoppers are committed by debt or contract. However, insofar as these committees bear serious responsibilities to institutions of higher learning, to their fields, and to their conception of science, they will probably not make their judgments merely according to the "feel" of validity or of its "ring of truth." It is "natural" for committee members to examine research problems in terms of how the problems (and they themselves) tie in with existing knowledge and theory, and to examine the research methods—intended or accomplished—according to how they (and themselves) relate to established operations for determining the validity of findings. It is not an easy decision for the judges, since to some extent and in some ways the success of the research (its completion and its validity) reflects upon them: they, too, are subject to group-defined norms. Hence, the questions they raise and the criticisms they offer tend to be typical of those found within their colleagueship or institution.

Although so-called *methodologists* tend to be more exacting and demanding than other audiences concerning how validation and reliability are assured, the logic underlying their expectations is not qualitatively different from that of other audiences whom the researcher is likely to encounter. Methodologists' logic is simply better articulated and grounded in conventional research procedures. The "ring of truth" is the same for all these audiences, except that the methodologists can identify the bells and have themselves been bell ringers. Those who have done field research in the manner we have described find that their validating procedures are not always or easily recognized by certain audiences. This may be as much the fault of the researcher in not making his procedures explicit as it is for an audience that may expect his procedures to be similar to those used by quantitative analysts.

An essential prerequisite to establishing credibilty with any audience is the researcher's conviction that what he is saying or writing is so. And this conviction rests upon necessary and credible procedures performed, as well as upon the sense of certainty that the observer did in fact see what he says he saw.

But what does this mean? It means that every proposition uttered—indeed, every declarative sentence—is a datum or a derivative of data, that the data are demonstrably empirical, and that they are empirically and logically related to the propositions stated. Even if the propositions are not particularly brilliant, they are grounded and the researcher has found no negative evidence bearing directly upon them. On this, at least, the researcher can rest his case. However, some audiences will not let him rest here; they require evidence or explicit affirmation of "validating procedures."

Some audiences must be fully assured that the researcher did pinpoint or check out every major proposition, that is, that each was derived from original field experience and from the data, was tested again with the data or with additional experience, and was also tested for logical consistency with every other major proposition. Quantative researchers characteristically demonstrate the validity of their findings through statistical tables and measures, and they therefore are likely to feel comfortable when defending their observations. Yet, if one were to ask them to defend the validity of the categories, one by one, upon which the tables and measures rest, they would be in essentially the same boat with the field researcher. Fortunately for them, most audiences do not question that far, conditioned as they are to the persuasive power of quantified evidence. The field researcher, however, may encounter some skepticism in those audiences who expect much quantified evidence from him.

Host verification

Credibility may be established with some audiences by showing or simply stating that at least the major propositions were tested or checked against the experiences and understandings of the hosts. If it was found that the propositions offered to the hosts did not empirically contradict their own understandings of their situation, then the researcher may convince audiences that he has a measure of validity—possibly a large measure. This mode of validating one's work does not require that the hosts actually concur in the propositions themselves, but that they recognize rather the validity of the grounds (events) upon which the propositions rest. But this procedure for achieving credibility with given audiences leads to another question which audiences may raise, bearing upon the repeatability or reliability of the work. Would another independent observer have seen or heard the same events, and reached the same conclusions?

For the field researcher whose view of social reality is one of infinite complexity, the only germane question is, *Would an independent observer make conceptual discoveries that empirically or logically invalidate his own?* That another observer—with or without the same general framework or perspective—might develop a very different analytic scheme, conceptual model, or metaphor is to be expected. Perceptual and conceptual selectivity must be taken for granted. Some identical and some different events would become data for other field observers; therefore, all independently developed data and analyses would necessarily be different. One or another analysis may be conceptually superior, but if any fails to contradict the original research, it must be regarded as supplementary or complementary.

A subsidiary question can also be posed: *Would another social science analyst, examining only the actual raw data (the ON's only) reach the same conclusions?* Here too, the answer would be the same. It is only when an independent analyst is given the original researcher's categories and propositions that he can possibly arrive at the same conclusions. Without these categories and linkages, another analyst—even if trained in the original researcher's own tradition—would create his own leads to follow and to develop.

Phenomenon recognition

The same or other audiences may pose a different order of questions not directly concerned with internal validation or with formal tests of reliability. They are knowledgeable about the phenomenon researched and themselves have had direct experiences with "it"—but elsewhere and under different circumstances and with different perspectives. These, too, may be difficult audiences with which to establish credibility, even if they are not methodologically sophisticated. They have their own direct and "real" experiences against which to test the validity of what our model researcher has said or written; they have worked—or still do work—in similar institutions or have had experiences as members of social movements. Now the researcher as communicator must rest his case upon the generality or universality of his propositions: *Do these people recognize the phenomenon?* Does what the researcher tells them call out in them a common experience? Even more important: *Does the researcher's analysis, which was probably based upon a different perspective or framework from theirs, actually help the audience explain—albeit in a new way—their own experiences?* If so, the researcher is virtually assured of credibility with this audience; for in a special sense, predictability and control, as well as generality are thereby indicated to them.

Yet, these audiences may find that what the researcher is saying—in part or whole—contradicts their own experiences and understandings. A lively dialogue may ensue with the audience offering negative evidence as a counterargument. But is it genuinely negative evidence? Evidence is negative only when it contradicts a hypothesis or proposition; otherwise it is, like any other data, positive for possibly another proposition or evidence of a sub-class or variant of the proposition stated in the first place but not accounted for in the researcher's analytic scheme. If the latter, the researcher will have learned something: most serious audiences make good teachers. In any event, if the researcher is secure in his own internal validation, and if he had done his comparative and historical analysis well, he will find little difficulty in defending his own propositional scheme. An additional reason for presenting to these audiences, then, is that they may greatly stimulate analysis, particularly on later phases of the research.

Letting Go: A Comment on Closure

Career exigencies and work styles, as well as research requirements figure prominently in the sequencing of research presentations, including the final presentation. Whether his current research is part of a larger endeavor or a highly circumscribed, one-time effort, the researcher will want to put final closure to it. If he is on an intellectual career course, other tasks will beckon him, although as an expert of sorts he may be called upon months and even years later to tell again, or anew, of his research. Whether undertaken hopefully, fearfully, or with a sense of boredom, the final writing poses a common problem: it relates to competence and to identification with some community of scholars.

There are researchers, on one hand, who literally rush into print, thinking they are ready despite cautionary cues signalled by their peers. For them, perhaps, publication *per se* is the name of the game, and the more the better. Or they publish because of or *in spite of* criticism. On the other hand, there are those who feel they are not intellectually ready, sometimes despite protestations of their colleagues to the contrary. They may put off closure for months—not stewing around, but doing other things; then later, having slowly digested audiences' comments, do their final writing. In these instances the structure of identification is different, as are the criteria for measuring competence. But in either case—the rush or the pause—the action is not a neurotic one. Somehow, each type is prepared to accept the consequences of his actions, including the possibility of having to blush years later when he is quoted for a work which now in his greater wisdom he would just as soon forget. Yet, at the time of final publication each had established credibility for himself and had "let go" of the work.

There are still other persons—not only researchers—for whom writing is a major problem, either because they are lacking in writing skills or because in some exaggerated sense they see the written word as a final, ineradicable fixing of their own intellectual identities; whereas in face-to-face talking about their work there is much room for immediate and tailored qualification and talking has an "off-the-record" quality. They find it extremely difficult to create options for themselves on when and how to end the work. Students, particularly for structural and career reasons, feel the weight of criticism from too many audiences, and in trying to satisfy all of them block their own efforts at closure. Indeed, some of their audiences appear to them so very knowledgeable and powerful on substance or method as to create a situation of coercion. Even their own colleagues can retard the necessary commitment, however altruistic their intentions. But in the end, it is the researcher—new or experienced—who must be his own judge on when and how to bring closure. To do this, he must himself be critically selective of criticism and then take a stand on his findings and methodology. Then he will "let go" and write what he understands to be reality, but even then, probably for limited audiences who will appreciate it—perhaps not all of it, but enough to establish a link with that community whose interests are met by his work.

A final word for purposes of emphasis: Having written his final report on his work, the researcher makes a commitment to the validity of the reality he created. He will have to stand by it even though later he will probably change, as will his conception of the reality he researched. But if he understands this, then he can also see final closure to his current work not as an end, but as a single bench mark in an intellectual career course. Also, then will he be able to smile when he reads Omar Khayyam's:

The moving finger writes, and having writ moves on . . .

Suggested Reading

Much of the literature on the communication of research is concerned with the ethical consequences of disclosure.

BARNES, J. A., "Some Ethical Problems in Modern Fieldwork," in William J. Filstead, *Qualitative Methodology: Firsthand Involvement with the Social World,* pp. 235–51. Chicago: Markham Publishing Company, 1970.

BECKER, HOWARD S., "Problems in the Publication of Field Studies," in Arthur J. Vidich et al., *Reflections on Community Studies,* pp. 267–84. New York: John Wiley & Sons, 1964. Also in McCall-Simmons, *Issues in Participant Observation: A Text and Reader,* pp. 260–76. Reading, Mass.: Addison-Wesley Publishing Co., 1969.

RAINWATER, LEE, and DAVID J. PITTMAN, "Ethical Problems in Studying a Politically Sensitive and Deviant Community," *Social Problems,* XIV (1967), 357–66. Also in McCall-Simmons, *Issues in Participant Observation,* pp. 276–88.

Our discussion on communicating the research is best illustrated through a bibliography which shows how essentially the "same" data (and some additional data and thought) were selectively written for different audiences.

GLASER, B., and A. STRAUSS, "The Social Loss of Dying Patients," *American Journal of Nursing,* LXIV (June 1964), 119–21.

———, "Dying on Time," *Trans-action* (May–June 1965), 27–31.

————, "Temporal Aspects of Dying as a Nonscheduled Status Passage," *American Journal of Sociology,* LXXI (1965), 45–59.

————, *A Time for Dying.* Chicago: Aldine Publishing Co., 1968.

STRAUSS, ANSELM, "Problems of Death and the Dying Patient," *Psychiatric Research Report* (February 1968), Chapter 15. Published by The American Psychiatric Association.

STRAUSS, ANSELM, and B. GLASER, "Patterns of Dying," in O. Brim et al. (eds.), *The Dying Patient.* New York: Russell Sage Foundation, 1970.

STRAUSS, A., B. GLASER, and J. QUINT, "The Non-Accountability of Terminal Care," *Hospitals,* XXXVIII (January 1964), 73–78.

Finally, a brief but good reading on the process of "letting go."

GLASER, BARNEY G., and ANSELM L. STRAUSS, *The Discovery of Grounded Theory.* Chicago: Aldine Publishing Co., 1967. See especially Chapter 9, pp. 223–35. (Originally published as "Discovery of Substantive Theory" in *American Behavioral Science* [1965], 5–12.)

Discusses bringing the research to a close, including the issue of conveying credibility and also the reader's responsibilities for judging credibility. All these topics bear on our discussion of presenting materials to audiences.

Epilogue

We have written this book for all students and professionals regardless of field, whose interest in social science has brought them to the point of wanting to do research themselves—not just any kind of research but that which naturally leads them to inquire into social events exactly as they are encountered. Although most students may be familiar with the findings of research gained through the field method, relatively few know much about the ways in which this form of inquiry is, or may be, conducted. Even many graduate students in the social and behavioral sciences who have taken courses in research methodology know little specifically of the operations involved in field research—little beyond knowing generally that such techniques as direct observation and interviewing are customarily employed.

In part, this lack of knowledge is due to the failure of most field researchers—mainly anthropologists and sociologists—to tell precisely or enough about how they work; in part, it is due to the failure of those who teach research to provide adequate instruction in the logic of this method and opportunity for students to work in this way. Hence, far from developing an affinity with research, those students who wish to be field researchers often come to wonder how the research models and processes they read about, or are taught, relate to their own observations and understandings of social life, and to their careers as well.

In attempting research while at school, these students have frequently had to compromise or abandon natural intellectual interests and skills in order to define problems and implement inquiries that are compatible only with more methodologically orthodox research models. It is for these persons that we have written, as well as for those who are new to research; also for instructors in research so that they may be encouraged to offer students equal opportunity to use field techniques in their term and thesis projects.

The authors have been teaching field research for many years on a general level in relatively large classrooms and more intensively for selected students. Additionally, we have been continually involved in our own joint and separate research projects. From these experiences, but mainy from the intensive coaching of graduate students, many of whom have had prior training in other research approaches, we have learned much about how students initially view research, and from whence their views originate.

Thus, we have learned that many graduate students sense a discrepancy or discontinuity between the established methods taught them and those they would normally use themselves, at least as applied to their own day-to-day observations of people and of ordinary human events. These students are certainly aware that formal methods of research are frequently the only, or the most suitable, ways of handling certain kinds of research problems. However, they wonder whether other problems—especially their own—can find equal operational expression in other research modes. Also, they are aware that their own informal methodological skills are relatively undeveloped and unsystematic; yet, somehow, the methodology presented to them appears *different in kind* from their own, rather than consisting simply of more sophisticated operations. What they wish and expect to learn are not only the orthodox methods of social research but operational skills which constitute elaborations and extensions of those they already have.

The authors take the view that the informal methods that students are inclined to use are not so different from the formal ones, though the ways in which the latter are taught and written about often make them appear quite different. Theoretically, all social science methods reflect the general requirements of Western science and cannot differ logically in kind from each other. Yet, the appearance of so great a difference can be traced to different perspectives taken by many methodologists both on the nature of human activity and on that of sciencing. These perspectives are reflected pedagogically in emphases given to three very closely linked components of contemporary thinking—substantive and methodological—in the social and behavioral sciences: mechanism as a model for human activity, standardized instrumentation in the operations of inquiry, and linearity in the design of research.

Mechanism and Instrumentation

For the the sake of brevity, we combine our discussion of the first two components. Mechanistic thinking about human action and human events generally, became fully established in modern times with acceptance of the Darwinian proposition that man is a species of animal. A number of logical implications drawn therefrom led not only to new ways of thinking about man but also to new ways of studying him. Man was linked to the "natural order" and viewed conveniently as subject to the same "natural laws" as those governing other natural objects. By discovering what "governing" meant, one was presumably discovering natural laws as these applied to man and to human events quite as to other objects and events. In keeping with the science of the time, these laws were to be viewed as determining, causal systems; therefore, human motions or actions were understandably made equivalent to determined behavior. This world view made it possible to objectify man in a new way and to model man after a machine or organism.

From these ideas came the development of comparative and physiological psychologies, and significantly, a stimulus-response framework to help explain human actions. Consistently and expectedly, there arose, without loss of mechanism as a model, an organismic sociology with emphasis upon the forms and functions of social relations. The stage was now set within the behavioral and social sciences for an effort to locate the "mainsprings" of human behavior—for psychology, generally within the organism; for sociology and anthropology, generally within the social-cultural environment. This type of thinking was explicitly or implicitly mechanistic, leading quite logically to the translation of "forces" into factors and variables to which "governing" or "responding" responsibilities might be ascribed.

Once established, this orientation led to a search for instrumentation to help discover and measure the stimulating forces and intervening mechanisms which determine response. Over time, a formidable array of instruments was developed. This effort was made understandable and acceptable, if not mandatory, in the context of a developing methodology which required accuracy, reliability and validity in the observation, control, measurement and analysis of variables.

Yet some deleterious consequences flowed from this effort, particularly as it affected generations of students who, driven by the logic and requirements of a "behavioral science," learned to define scientific problems appreciably in terms of the availability and capability of instruments favored or mandated in their time. The instruments—indeed virtually the entire process of thinking about research—rather quickly took on formidable qualities independent of the persons using them. Many students accepted the mandate and fused their own ideas with prevailing thought on the nature of sciencing. And why not, considering the relatively systematic discrediting, since the 1920s, of man's ability to make valid observations and inferences of his own? Was it not established that man was subject to error, bias, irrationality; and that his performance through "insight" was no match for independent, highly reliable instrumentation?

For an indeterminate number of other students, the pathway to "hard social science" was neither exciting nor tempting: they were reluctant to transform, or even abandon altogether, their research interests simply because they were "not amenable" to what had become orthodox instrumentation. However, all too frequently, they discovered it was expedient in the context of graduate or professional education to prepare research primarily as an exercise in the demonstration of competence with instruments. Indeed, it became understood that competence in a given substantive area was demonstrable through competence in specified operations. (We are reminded of the visiting graduate student who, when clearly asked about the substance of his dissertation, replied "I'm doing an analysis of variance.")

Linearity in Research Design

In the social and behavioral sciences, the most commonly used model for telling and writing about research takes the form of a narrative—a linear series of thoughts, operations, and outcomes—beginning with a statement of the problem, followed by a description of procedural design as intention, then by a description of actual operations, and ending with an itemization and discussion of findings. The operational portion of the narrative is also linear or sequential: sampling first, then data gathering, followed by data analysis. The linearity and the categories of the narrative suggest which of the total events experienced in the actual execution of the research are to be included in the final telling of the research story: events from among the countless acts comprising the research, from among the many "factors" taken into account, and from the myriad contingencies which impinged upon the research throughout its course. The narrator orders the selected events sequentially, more or less in terms of the linear model. While we have suggested that the research may not at all have gone as described, there is yet another position from which the research narrative can be viewed.

Aside from its apparent consistency with the mandates of science, the research narrative is important as a piece of communication. Addressed to future and contemporary audiences, this form is convenient for researchers' use. Moreover, the narrative is useful because it provides order and parsimony: it identifies problem, method and findings conveniently and provides a form for creating the credibility of a linear, logical, and causal relation among them. For these reasons the model is deeply embedded in the practices of educational institutions and professional research organizations. Schools teach that scientific work proceeds in such a fashion; scholarly journals favor research writing that follows this form; major funding agencies practically demand that proposals be prepared according to the requirements of the model (often requiring "anticipated" results in place of actual "findings").

We suggest that research itself involves a different organization of activity than research writing, and has a different social locus. Its locus is "in the field," in the special relation of the researcher to his object of inquiry, whatever his method. Research has mainly to do with the process of inquiry; research writing has to do with the process of communication— and for all practical purposes each has its own "field." This distinction is important because our writing has been concerned with a mode of work grounded in research experience rather than in the experience of writing about research.

Sociologically put, it is not the research which confers upon the researcher his status as a scientist; status primarily comes from the groups and institutions to which the researcher addresses his publications. This derivation of status helps account for the durability of the narrative model; but it does not fully account for the researcher's actual performance in the field. There, he finds or constructs his method as required by the peculiarities of his specific inquiry, and the conditions of the research field. Later, in describing what he did, he finds or constructs another method as required by professional communication and by the special features of his audiences. This suggests that "two methodologies" are linked through the researcher's performance in each field. If the reader cannot quite accept the idea of two methods then perhaps he can accept the following: One method is addressed to the object of inquiry as guided by the requirements of the audience to whom the findings later will be reported; the second (narrative model) is addressed to professional audiences, guided by the events of the inquiry already concluded. The two representations of method simply alternate as background and foreground depending upon time, location, and audience, or point of reference.

No necessary conflict is involved in dealing with these two methods, although students and other novices in research may sense a discrepancy or experience conflict when taking linearity literally, or when teachers of methodology insist upon linearity as a practice. There are two reasons for the lack of conflict between acts of inquiry and acts of writing.

First, the audiences which read research do not require full disclosure of all research actions nor of their true ordering. They are concerned only with the disclosure of those activities which could plausibly be related to the attained results, and which other researchers would need to know to perform work yielding similar results. That the next researcher probably could not get the same results from *only* the same actions, and in exactly the *same* order, causes no apparent concern.

A second reason for lack of conflict is that, aside from communication about what he will do or has done, the researcher has very few field requirements with which he need be concerned, the linear model notwithstanding. The order and types of activities to which he must attend are simply those that facilitate his inquiry. These need have neither direct relation to the future constructed narrative nor to the design he may have developed to obtain funds or institutional license for doing the research.

The requirements of research as they relate to science are simple enough: the researcher must deal with phenomena which have empirical referents; he must provide evidence for whatever constructs are developed about the phenomenon, and the evidence must be empirically and logically related to the operations performed upon the object of inquiry. The operations need *not* follow any given model: a maximum of operational maneuverability is fully available to the researcher. Some research operations occur in linear, progressive fashion; many occur simultaneously; while others occur "regressively" as when someone towards the end of his study discovers his "true" problem and its associated hypotheses. This may not be how methodology is taught or written about, but *it is how original non-replicative research takes place*. Originality has no absolute, programmatic model to work from; it has its "own ways" and a logic necessarily consistent only with the general requirements of order and communication.

Having said the foregoing, we are tempted to undertake field studies of ongoing social science research projects. We imagine that many of our findings would resemble the kinds of dialogue which occur when "true colleagues" swap yarns about their research. Such insiders tell of casual observations that proved more critical or fruitful than the planned, systematic ones; of carefully prepared "designs" and expectations mutilated by unforseeable events; and of initial hypotheses that subsequently proved to be too foolish for later disclosure. Surely, even the most skilled and experienced researchers would tell how "disorderly" some research operations can be; indeed, how often certain "operations" are little more than random motion in search of meaning.

Our efforts in this book were intended to alert the novice in research to these very probabilities and to indicate the kinds of thinking he might engage in to make of this mode of research a positive experience despite its difficulties. Many novices do not see these difficulties until their data have piled up quite beyond their control. Then they begin to realize that the field research they "knew" through reading alone was deceptively simple. Only much later, when the novice has achieved an acute self-consciousness about his actual research performance in the field—when he has made his work systematic, organized, and sustained, and particularly when he has developed an analytic style—he will see that these properties of field research are a quantum jump beyond the informal inclinations and skills with which he began.

Strategy, Common Sense, and Ethics

A researcher's interest in some social phenomenon, and even his theoretical framework and perspective, will give him little or no understanding as to how he may proceed to study it; these provide him only with a measure of conceptual order. While the field method does not require operational design in the same sense as it may in other research methods, it nevertheless requires sets of strategies and implementing tactics to meet the requirements of getting data and of analyzing them. Otherwise, there are considerable waste of time and energy and probably some fateful errors in conduct. By "strategy" we mean recognizing, planning, and organizing ways of dealing with the major requirements—seeing, hearing, understanding—of the research. Since the object of inquiry is simultaneously substance and host, a multitude of tactics are necessary to implement strategic decisions. The tactics of conduct take many forms, sometimes differing little from common sense and good manners. At times, in the classroom, we blush at finding it necessary to tell our fully grown students to say "please" and "thank you," and not to "come on too strong." Indeed, if common sense and good manners can "go without saying," then we need not have written as much as we have; they are *not* so common, and they are assuredly vital to field research.

In writing about strategies and tactics as conscious and organized activities, they may appear quite Machiavellian in the sense of appearing manipulative. Yet, unquestionably, we want our hosts to do exactly what we wish them to do, and the tactics we use make it possible for them to do it. However, also unquestionable is the moral requirement to maintain the relative comfort and security of the host. Therefore, if his means to research are benign and his purposes good, the researcher can regard himself as expressing both intelligence and human concern. He needs both strategy and morality. The first without the second is cruel; the second without the first is ineffectual.

Index